MW01168511

The Doctor Sebi Alkaline Diet Cookbook

A Complete Doctor Sebi Diet Guideline with 250 Healthy Recipes to Balance Your PH and Keep Healthy (3-Week Meal Plan Included)

Nauger Loaney

Table of Content

Chapter 6: Grains 33

Chapter 7: Salads 45

Chapter 8: Snacks 59

Chapter 9: Soups and Stews. 69

Chapter 10: Desserts 83

Chapter 11: Smoothies.......... 92

Introduction

Making positive lifestyle changes, especially when it comes to diet, can keep you healthy and strong both physically and mentally. A lesser-known diet that is quickly gaining popularity today is the Dr. Sebi Alkaline diet.

This book will be your resource for everything you need to know about this diet and how you can follow it. It will take you through all the wonderful benefits and will give you a step-by-step guide on how to make this diet a part of your life. The valuable insights in this book will help you reap all the plentiful benefits of the Dr. Sebi Alkaline diet.

Perhaps, the greatest part of the Dr. Sebi Alkaline diet is that it is capable of whole-body cell rejuvenation, which happens through the elimination of toxic waste by alkalizing your blood. It sounds complicated, but the process is simple once you get the hang of it.

Based on the Afro Bio-Mineral Balance Theory that was invented by Alfredo Darrington Bowman (Dr. Sebi), this diet was designed to protect your body from diseases and ailments. Although Dr. Sebi is not a certified medical doctor, many people have sworn by his techniques and his diet has received real high praise from those who live by it. The overall point of adapting to the Dr. Sebi diet is to eliminate the need for Western medicine. When your body can function so well on its own, it will not need medicine or any other assistance. Your natural body processes will keep you healthy.

Dr. Sebi stated that your body is affected by diseases because of a build-up of mucus in certain areas of your body. As an example, he believed that pneumonia occurs because of mucus build-up in the lungs. His solution was to alkalize your body, because mucus cannot survive in an alkalized state. Throughout his years practicing this unique version of medicine, many skeptics argued that these techniques were not real. However, many people swear by this diet and have gone on to live healthy, happy lives while abiding by the diet's guidelines.

The Dr. Sebi diet is a successful and comprehensive lifestyle plan. While on this diet, you will be eating from a list of approved vegetables, fruits, grains, seeds, nuts, oils, and herbs. Animal products are not a part of the diet, as they do not support the alkalizing process the diet is meant to achieve. To fully heal your body, Dr. Sebi recommended you follow the diet for the rest of your life.

Chapter 1: The Benefits

One of the biggest health benefits you will experience while on the Dr. Sebi diet is that of overall health improvement. All the nutrition you will be receiving in this diet is from plant-based ingredients. Without the incorporation of animal products, you will be maintaining a diet that promotes great heart health and cholesterol health. In a study that included 65,000 participants, those who consumed seven or more servings of fruits and vegetables daily experienced a 25 to 31% lower instance of developing heart disease (Davidson 2019).

Dr. Sebi always placed a very strong emphasis on the plant-based aspect of the diet, claiming it was why this diet was so different (and better) than other diets. You will be consuming high amounts of fiber, minerals, and plant compounds, all of which will aid your digestion, increase your brain function, and keep your skin, hair, and nails healthy and vibrant.

Diets, like the Dr. Sebi diet, that are known for including plenty of fruits and vegetables are also known for reducing the risk of inflammation in the body. Whenever your body is experiencing inflammation of any kind, you tend to feel physically unwell. Your joints and bones suffer because inflammation causes aches and pains, and your internal systems will feel fatigued and won't operate as they should. When there is inflammation present, your immune system suffers as well, as it can't prevent or recover from different types of illnesses and diseases.

When you are eating pure—or whole—foods, that means you are getting the most nutritious elements of each ingredient. Without any additives or processed ingredients, you can be sure that your diet is pure and completely free of toxins. This is exactly what Dr. Sebi wanted when he created this diet: a pure and toxin-free body. To achieve this, he created a diet that is full of plenty of nutritious food that doesn't rely on the standard Western ingredients that taste good but are so bad for you.

If you are looking for a diet that promotes overall body and mind health, the Dr. Sebi Alkaline diet is for you. Its benefits are meant to work for the long-term, not the short-term. Because it is a more permanent solution, the diet is seen as a lifestyle rather than a fad. It is something you can continue to maintain as you age, keeping your body functioning at its prime. This diet plan ages with you without the need to change as your body changes. This diet is suitable for all types of people, both young and old. Even if you already have illnesses and diseases, it can help to purify your system and potentially alleviate some of your symptoms.

Chapter 2: Food Principles

The Dr. Sebi diet is one that is very particular. Yet, Dr. Sebi created the detailed guideline below that will allow you to easily follow the diet the way it was intended. While it might seem intimidating at first, nothing ventured is nothing gained. All you have to do is follow the path laid out for you.

For many, this diet is a very big change, so all changes away from your current diet should be made gradually. You should not expect to memorize or adhere to all of these rules overnight. If you want to make the commitment, start slowly.

Eight Rules

1. **Rule One:** You must only eat the foods listed in the Dr. Sebi nutritional guide (see below).

2. **Rule Two:** Drink one gallon of water daily.

3. **Rule Three:** Take Dr. Sebi's supplements an hour before you take any other medication(s).

4. **Rule Four:** There are no animal products allowed while on this diet.

5. **Rule Five:** There is no alcohol allowed while on this diet.

6. **Rule Six:** You must refrain from eating wheat products, and instead, you can supplement with whole grains.

7. **Rule Seven:** Avoid using a microwave to heat your food because it will kill essential nutrients.

8. **Rule Eight:** Avoid eating canned or seedless fruits.

Nutritional Guide

Vegetables	Amaranth Greens, Avocado, Bell Peppers, Chayote, Cucumber, Dandelion Greens, Garbanzo Beans, Izote, Kale, Lettuce (all except iceberg), Mushrooms, Nopales, Okra, Olives, Onions, Sea Vegetables, Squash, Tomato (only cherry and plum), Tomatillo, Turnip Greens, Zucchini, Watercress, Verdolaga, Wild Arugula
Fruits	Apples, Bananas (small), Berries (all except cranberries), Elderberries, Cantaloupe, Cherries, Currants, Dates, Figs, Grapes (seeded), Limes, Mango, Melons, Orange, Papayas, Peaches, Pears, Plums, Prickly Pear, Prunes, Raisins, Soft Jelly Coconuts, Soursops, Tamarind
Natural Herbal Teas	Burdock, Chamomile, Elderberry, Fennel, Ginger, Raspberry, Tila
Grains	Amaranth, Fonio, Kamut, Quinoa, Rye, Spelt, Tef, Wild Rice
Nuts and Seeds (including butters)	Hemp, Raw Sesame, Tahini, Walnuts
Oils	Olive Oil (not cooked), Coconut Oil (not cooked, Grapeseed Oil, Sesame Oil, Hemp Seed Oil, Avocado Oil
Spices and Seasonings: Mild	Basil, Bay Leaves, Cloves, Dill, Oregano, Savory, Sweet Basil, Tarragon, Thyme
Spices and Seasonings: Pungent	Achiote, Cayenne, Onion Powder, Habanero, Sage
Spices and Seasonings: Salty	Pure Sea Salt, Powdered Granulated Seaweed, Kelp
Spices and Seasonings: Sweet	Pure Agave Syrup, Date Sugar

Weight Loss: Is It Possible?

Unlike most diet plans, the Dr. Sebi diet was not designed with weight loss in mind. However, while on the Dr. Sebi diet, you can potentially lose weight, but there are no guarantees. Generally, weight loss happens when you burn more calories than you consume. Because it is a diet that is meant to cleanse your system from the inside out, it is possible that you can become leaner and lose some weight.

The positive part about the Dr. Sebi diet that works in favor of weight loss is the rejection of the typical Western diet. This means that it discourages you from eating any foods that are high in fats, sugars, and other processed or artificial ingredients. This makes you a lot healthier in the long run and, in turn, it might end up slimming you down if you are used to eating a lot of processed foods on a regular basis.

Overall, however, this is not a diet that is built on the idea of quick weight loss or muscle making. It is about transforming your whole health and body, which could mean losing weight. For example, during a 12-month study, 65 people were instructed to follow a diet of unlimited whole foods (no added preservatives) and low-fat plant-based options (this is a very similar basis to the Dr. Sebi diet). The results found that these individuals lost a significant amount of weight as compared to others who were not eating this way (Davidson 2019). Another finding from the study showed that after six months of eating this way, participants were able to lose an average of 26.6 pounds, while those in the control group only lost an average of 3.5 pounds, which is a very significant difference.

If you want to detox your body while simultaneously losing weight, the Dr. Sebi diet can assist you with this. You must be willing to change some of your other lifestyle habits in the process, such as exercising more and adopting other healthy behavioral habits.

Most of the foods you will be eating on the Dr. Sebi diet are low in calories, which is great if weight loss happens to be a goal you have in mind. Just make sure that you are not making this your main goal. Think about detoxing first and losing weight second. Even while eating the healthy and approved foods on the Dr. Sebi diet, you need to keep moderation in mind. An abundance of these ingredients will result in a higher consumption of calories and the potential to gain weight.

Chapter 3: Foods to Avoid

Because the diet is so calculated and particular, you need to be aware of certain foods that you are to avoid while on the Dr. Sebi diet. These rules are in place to help your body detoxify. If you were to consume them, you would be going against the process of alkalizing that makes up the foundation of your diet.

Use this reference whenever you are unsure about whether a specific food is part of the diet or needs to be skipped. Even though there are quite a few foods that you cannot eat, there are just as many foods that you can supplement them with. While on a plant-based diet, flavor is going to make a huge difference in the way that your meals taste. Anything well-seasoned with the approved list of spices and herbs is going to make you forget about these off-limit foods that you might crave.

Remember, though: Having cravings is natural when you are on any type of diet, but they will pass the longer that you resist them. By nourishing your body with other foods that are just as delicious and filling, the cravings that you experience will soon shift—you will find yourself wanting the healthy, plant-based options instead of the typical junk food snacks you desire. With the Dr. Sebi diet, there is a form of self-discipline that must be mastered. Try not to be hard on yourself as you make this transition. If you go into this slowly, your body will eventually get used to it, your cravings will subside, and you will feel better than ever.

Canned Fruits and Vegetables

When you consume fruits and vegetables, it is always best to go for the fresh options. The canning process typically eliminates the nutrients in fruits and vegetables because preservatives are added to make sure the food doesn't go bad. Even though you can eat the same canned fruits and vegetables as the ones you will find in the produce section, you will not be getting the same nutritional value from them.

Seedless Fruit

This one might confuse you because eating plenty of fruit is encouraged while on the Dr. Sebi diet. Seedless fruit is an exception because it eliminates a lot of genetic diversity in the fruit. This means that a fruit might contain certain pesticides and have the potential to be cloned, so you are not consuming the healthiest version of the fruit.

Eggs

While eggs provide you with protein, they also contain a chemical called lecithin. This chemical gets converted into a compound chemical inside of your gut that is called TMAO. In excess, TMAO is thought to lead to an increased risk of heart attacks and strokes.

Dairy

While dairy is supposed to make your bones strong, it also becomes a top source of saturated fat in the typical American diet. With an abundance of this kind of fat, you are putting yourself at a higher risk of developing type 2 diabetes, heart disease, and various cancers.

Red Meat

A lot of red meat is high in saturated fat. When you consume too much of it, you are raising your cholesterol—the exact opposite effect that you are striving for while on the Dr. Sebi diet. When this happens, you are putting yourself at risk of heart disease.

Soy Products

While a lot of diets promote the consumption of soy, it turns out that it isn't the healthiest option to eat in abundance. Especially while you are plant-based, you might think that soy is going to become a natural alternative. Soy actually contains estrogen-like compounds that are thought to promote the growth of certain cancer cells.

Processed Foods

It has already been mentioned, but you are going to eliminate all processed foods from your diet because they are filled with chemicals and preservatives. Consuming these foods will create toxins in your body that it cannot use. Plus, these processed foods are the kind that tend to be high in saturated fat and sugar—both of which are not recommended while eating the Dr. Sebi diet.

Chapter 4: FAQs

Q: Is it possible to get enough protein in a plant-based diet?

A: The answer is yes, you can still get plenty of protein while adhering the Dr. Sebi diet. Most people are convinced that eating meat is the only way to obtain a decent amount of protein, but there are much healthier sources of protein available. Some examples include lentils, chickpeas, hempseed, most beans, peas, wild rice, breads made from sprouted grains, and amaranth.

As you get used to eating a plant-based diet, you will figure out ways to incorporate more protein into each of your meals. The best way for you to discover these combinations is to step outside of your comfort zone—make different recipes from this cookbook until you find your new favorites. If you are still struggling to get enough protein, you always have the option of taking supplements to enrich your diet. Several individuals who are on plant-based diets are known for taking vitamins to further aid their nutrition needs.

Q: Is the Dr. Sebi diet too restricting?

A: Many people take notice of the fact that there are quite a few rules surrounding this diet, but they are all in place for good reasons. While there are certain foods that you are instructed to avoid entirely, this is because those foods will add toxins to your system that make it harder for your body to function in its alkalized state.

Because the typical American diet is full of foods that are not very nutritious, it can seem like a harsh change when switching over to the Dr. Sebi diet. Being mindful of the fact that you can transition into this diet is the key. If you make this transition slowly, you won't feel like you are entirely restricting yourself. As your body adjusts to your new eating habits, you will start wanting to eat all the foods in the guideline and won't feel restricted at all.

Q: Is the diet safe?

A: The Dr. Sebi diet is typically safe for most individuals. To get the most accurate answer, a consultation with your physician would be the best option. There are many diets out there that people maintain that are very similar to the Dr. Sebi diet—many plant-based vegans and vegetarians swear by their diets. While plant-based diets all differ in terms of what they focus on, the Dr. Sebi diet is within the same ranks as them.

Any diet needs to be taken on with caution and moderation. The Dr. Sebi diet is no different. If you change your habits to the extreme, you are going to be met with poor results. Your body is full of systems that need to adapt to any changes. So, the Dr. Sebi diet is quite safe, just proceed with slow steps.

Q: Will this diet make me tired or lead to low energy?

A: No, you will feel more energized. When you are actually being nourished by the food you eat, you are going to feel it in every part of your body. Your mind will feel clearer, your endurance will rise, and you will have a general feeling of contentment as you move through your day. The sluggish feeling that you often reach before the day ends stems from your lack of nutrition. The Dr. Sebi diet increases the nutrition you put in your body.

Q: Will the meals become boring because of the restrictions?

A: The great thing about all of the recipes you will find in this cookbook is that they offer plenty of variety. Even though you are eliminating a lot of ingredients that you would typically eat in an average diet, you are being taught several different methods of making your food taste great. You will also find that eating whole, plant-based meals is a lot more satisfying than filling your cravings with junk food.

Chapter 5: Vegetables

Basil Mushroom and Lettuce Burgers

Prep time: 15 minutes | Cook time: 20 minutes | Serves 2

2 cups portobello mushroom caps	½ teaspoon cayenne
1 sliced avocado	1 teaspoon oregano
1 sliced plum tomatoes	2 teaspoons basil
1 cup torn lettuce	3 tablespoons olive oil
1 cup purslane	

1. Preheat the oven to 425ºF (220ºC).
2. Remove the mushroom stems and cut off ½ inch slice from the top slice, as if slicing a bun.
3. Mix onion powder, cayenne, oregano, olive oil and basil thoroughly in a medium bowl.
4. Cover a baking sheet with foil and brush with grape seed oil to avoid sticking.
5. Put mushroom caps on the baking sheet and brush them with the prepared marinade. Marinate for 10 minutes before cooking.
6. Bake for 10 minutes until golden brown then flip. Continue baking for 10 more minutes.
7. Lay out the mushroom cap on a serving dish. This will serve as the bottom for the mushroom burger. on it layer the sliced avocado, tomatoes, lettuce, and purslane.
8. Cover the burger with another mushroom cap. Repeat steps 7 and 8 with the remaining mushrooms and vegetables.
9. Serve and enjoy.

Per Serving
calories: 375 | fat: 35.6g | protein: 5.0g carbs: 15.1g | fiber: 8.9g

Zoodles with Tomato-Avocado Sauce

Prep time: 10minutes | Cook time: 15 to 20 minutes | Serves 3

3 medium zucchini	3 tablespoons olive oil
1½ cup cherry tomatoes	Juice of 1 key lemon
1 avocado	1 tablespoon spring water
2 sliced green onions	Pure sea salt, to taste
$1/_3$ cup fresh leaf parsley	Cayenne, to taste
1 clove garlic	

1. Preheat the oven to 400ºF (205ºC).
2. Cover a baking sheet with a piece of parchment paper.
3. Put the cherry tomatoes on the covered baking sheet. Drizzle with 1 tablespoon olive oil and season with pure sea salt and cayenne.
4. Bake the tomatoes for about 15 to 20 minutes until they start to split.
5. Add quartered avocado, torn parsley leaves, sliced green onions, garlic, spring water, key lemon juice and ½ teaspoon pure sea salt to a food processor. Blend until it achieves a creamy consistency. If the sauce is too thick, add more spring water.
6. Cut off the ends of the zucchini. Using a spiralizer, make zucchini noodles.
7. Mix the zucchini noodles with the prepared avocado sauce.
8. Divide into 3 small bowls and serve with cherry tomatoes.
9. Enjoy the zoodles with the sauce!

Per Serving
calories: 270 | fat: 23.9g | protein: 3.8g carbs: 14.8g | fiber: 6.9g

Avocado Spelt Pasta

Prep time: 20 minutes | Cook time: 0 minutes | Serves 4

4 cups cooked spelt pasta
1 medium diced avocado
2 cups halved cherry tomatoes
1 minced fresh basil
1 teaspoon agave syrup
1 tablespoon key lime juice
¼ cup olive oil

1. Place the cooked pasta in a large bowl.
2. Add diced avocado, halved cherry tomatoes, and minced basil into the bowl.
3. Stir all the ingredients until well combined.
4. Whisk agave syrup, olive oil, pure sea salt and key lime juice in a separate bowl.
5. Pour it over the pasta and stir until well combined.
6. Serve immediately.

Per Serving
calories: 395 | fat: 22.0g | protein: 5.4g
carbs: 47.7g | fiber: 11.0g

Lettuce and Zucchini Hummus Wrap

Prep time: 10 minutes | Cook time: 8 minutes | Serves 2

½ cup iceberg lettuce
1 zucchini, sliced
2 cherry tomatoes, sliced
2 spelt flour tortillas
4 tablespoons
homemade hummus
¼ teaspoon salt
⅛ teaspoon cayenne pepper
1 tablespoon grapeseed oil

1. Take a grill pan, grease it oil and let it preheat over medium-high heat setting.
2. Meanwhile, place zucchini slices in a large bowl, sprinkle with salt and cayenne pepper, drizzle with oil and then toss until coated.
3. Arrange zucchini slices on the grill pan and then cook for 2 to 3 minutes per side until developed grill marks.
4. Assemble tortillas and for this, heat the tortilla on the grill pan until warm and develop grill marks and spread 2 tablespoons hummus over each tortilla.
5. Distribute grilled zucchini slices over the tortillas, top with lettuce and tomato slices, and then wrap tightly.
6. Serve straight away.

Per Serving
calories: 265 | fat: 5.2g | protein: 8.4g
carbs: 34.6g | fiber: 4.9g

Basil Spinach Pesto Pasta

Prep time: 10 minutes | Cook time: 10 minutes | Serves 4

2 cups dried gluten-free pasta
3 cups packed baby spinach
½ cup packed fresh basil
3 tablespoons
avocado oil
3 tablespoons walnut pieces
1 to 2 garlic cloves, peeled
⅛ teaspoon sea salt

1. Bring a pot of water to a boil and cook the pasta according to the package instructions. Drain, transfer to a large bowl, and set aside.
2. In a food processor, combine the spinach, basil, oil, walnuts, garlic, and salt and pulse for 20 to 30 seconds, until the desired consistency is reached. Toss the pesto with the cooked pasta and serve.

Per Serving
calories: 321 | fat: 15.1g | protein: 5.9g
carbs: 42.2g | fiber: 6.8g

Mushroom and Bell Pepper Fajitas

Prep time: 10 minutes | Cook time: 10 minutes | Serves 3

6 tortillas
3 large portobello mushrooms
1 onion
2 bell peppers
1 teaspoon onion powder

1 teaspoon habanero pepper
⅛ teaspoon cayenne powder
Juice of ½ key lime
1 tablespoon grape seed oil

1. Rinse the portobello mushrooms and remove their stems. Cut into $1/_3$-inch slices.
2. Cut onion and bell peppers into thin slices.
3. Add grape seed oil to a large skillet and warm on medium heat. Add sliced onions and bell peppers and cook for 2 minutes.
4. Place sliced mushrooms and seasonings into the pan. Cook for 7 to 8 minutes, stirring occasionally. Remove from the heat.
5. Grab a small pan, put tortillas on it and warm for 30 to 60 seconds on each side.
6. Place the filling mixture into the tortillas' center and sprinkle the key lime juice over the vegetables.
7. Serve and enjoy.

Per Serving
calories: 401 | fat: 10.8g | protein: 11.4g
carbs: 66.0g | fiber: 6.9g

Kale and Avocado

Prep time: 5 minutes | Cook time: 0 minutes | Serves 2

1 bundle of kale, cut into thin strips
1 small white onion, peeled, chopped
12 cherry tomatoes,

chopped
1 tablespoon salt
1 avocado, peeled, pitted, sliced

1. Take a large bowl, place kale strips in it, sprinkle with salt, and then massage for 2 minutes.
2. Cover the bowl with a plastic wrap or its lid, let it rest for a minimum of 30 minutes, and then stir in onion and tomatoes until well combined.
3. Let the salad sit for 5 minutes, add avocado slices, and then serve.

Per Serving
calories: 145 | fat: 10.6g | protein: 2.9g
carbs: 12.5g | fiber: 4.6g

Bell Pepper and Mushroom Spelt Noodles

Prep time: 5 minutes | Cook time: 10 minutes | Serves 2

2 cups cooked spelt noodles
½ of medium green bell pepper, cored, sliced
½ of medium red bell pepper, cored, sliced
1 medium white onion, cored, sliced

½ cup sliced mushrooms
$2/_3$ teaspoon salt
¼ teaspoon onion powder
$1/_3$ teaspoon cayenne pepper
1 key lime juiced
1 tablespoon sesame oil

1. Take a large skillet pan, place it over medium heat, add oil and when hot, add all the vegetables and cook for 3 to 5 minutes until tender-crisp.
2. Add all the spices, drizzle with lime juice, stir until mixed, and then cook for 1 minute.
3. Add noodles, toss until well mixed and then cook for 2 to 3 minutes until hot.
4. Serve straight away.

Per Serving
calories: 331 | fat: 10.8g | protein: 10.1g
carbs: 47.9g | fiber: 3.9g

Chickpea, Bell Pepper and Mushroom Curry

Prep time: 5 minutes | Cook time: 12 minutes | Serves 2

1 cup cooked chickpea	mushrooms
1 small white onion, peeled, diced	8 cherry tomatoes, chopped
½ of medium green bell pepper, cored, chopped	½ teaspoon salt
	¼ teaspoon cayenne pepper
1 cup diced	1 teaspoon grapeseed oil

1. Take a medium skillet pan, place it over medium heat, add oil and when hot, add onion, tomatoes, and bell pepper and then cook for 2 minutes.
2. Add chickpeas and mushrooms, season with and cayenne pepper, stir until combined, and switch heat to medium-low level and then simmer for 10 minutes until cooked, covering the pan with its lid.
3. Serve straight away.

Per Serving

calories: 195 | fat: 8.6g | protein: 5.6g carbs: 25.6g | fiber: 5.5g

Cucumber and Lentil Pasta

Prep time: 5 minutes | Cook time: 0 minutes | Serves 1 to 2

⅓ cup avocado oil	leaves, chopped
2 tablespoons apple cider vinegar	1 cup cooked lentils
2 tablespoons water	1 cup cooked green lentil elbow pasta
½ teaspoon dried oregano	½ cup unpeeled chopped cucumber
¼ to ½ teaspoon sea salt	¼ cup thinly sliced onion
¼ teaspoon ground black pepper	5 to 10 small basil leaves, for garnish (optional)
2 small fresh basil	

1. In a small bowl, whisk together the avocado oil, vinegar, water, oregano, salt, pepper, and basil until everything is well combined. Adjust the seasonings to your preference.
2. Add the cooked lentils and pasta to the serving bowl, and gently toss them together so they are evenly distributed. Top with the cucumbers and onions, drizzle with the dressing, and garnish with the basil leaves (if using).
3. Transfer to 1 large or 2 small plates and enjoy.

Per Serving

calories: 606 | fat: 34.3g | protein: 13.3g carbs: 64.1g | fiber: 14.3g

Baked Sage Mushrooms

Prep time: 10 minutes | Cook time: 30 minutes | Serves 2

2 cups portobello mushrooms, destemmed	sage
	⅔ teaspoon thyme
⅔ teaspoon minced onion	⅔ tablespoon key lime juice
⅔ teaspoon minced	2 tablespoons alkaline soy sauce

1. Switch on the oven, then set it to 400ºF (205ºC) and let it preheat.
2. Take a baking dish and then arrange mushroom caps in it, cut side up.
3. Take a small bowl, place remaining ingredients in it, stir until mixed, brush the mixture over inside and outside mushrooms, and then let them marinate for 15 minutes.
4. Bake the mushrooms for 30 minutes, flipping halfway, and then serve.

Per Serving

calories: 34 | fat: 0.4g | protein: 4.4g carbs: 5.2g | fiber: 1.3g

Barbecue Sprout Bean Salsa Chili

Prep time: 5 minutes | Cook time: 25 minutes | Serves 4

Cooking spray
1 small onion, chopped
1 cup diced red bell pepper
2 garlic cloves, finely chopped
2 cups sprouted beans, black, kidney, or pinto
1 (14.5-ounce / 411-g) can diced tomatoes

2 tablespoons barbecue sauce
1 (8-ounce / 227-g) jar organic pasta sauce
¼ cup organic salsa, mild, medium, or hot
¼ cup organic fresh cilantro
Dash chili powder
Dash ground cumin

1. Spray a medium-size pot with cooking spray. Set it over medium heat. Add the onions and sauté for 5 minutes, or until they're soft and slightly caramelized.
2. Add the bell pepper, garlic, sprouted beans, tomatoes, Homemade Barbecue Sauce, pasta sauce, salsa, cilantro, chili powder, and cumin. Stir to combine. Simmer for 20 minutes.
3. Serve immediately.

Per Serving
calories: 459 | fat: 6.8g | protein: 23.8g
carbs: 78.8g | fiber: 20.4g

Okra and Tomato Curry

Prep time: 5 minutes | Cook time: 10 minutes | Serves 2

1½ cup okra
8 cherry tomatoes, chopped
1 medium onion, peeled, sliced
¾ cup vegetable broth, homemade
6 teaspoons spice mix

¼ teaspoon salt
½ tablespoon grapeseed oil
¼ teaspoon cayenne pepper
¾ cup tomato sauce, alkaline
6 tablespoons soft-jelly coconut milk

1. Take a large skillet pan, place it over medium heat, add oil and warm, add onion, and then cook for 5 minutes until golden brown.
2. Add spice mix, add remaining ingredients into the pan except for okra, stir until mixed, and then bring the mixture to a simmer.
3. Add okra, stir until mixed, and then cook for 10 to 15 minutes over medium-low heat setting until cooked.
4. Serve straight away.

Per Serving
calories: 138 | fat: 8.5g | protein: 4.1g
carbs: 14.9g | fiber: 5.5g

Broccoli and Carrot Bake

Prep time: 10 minutes | Cook time: 30 minutes | Serves 2

1 pound (454 g) broccoli, cut into bite-size pieces
4 carrots, peeled and sliced
3 garlic heads, cloves peeled and chopped, or 3 tablespoons minced

2 teaspoons lemon zest
1 teaspoon sea salt
¼ teaspoon mustard powder
1 cup vegetable broth
2 tablespoons coconut oil

1. Preheat the oven to 400ºF (205ºC).
2. In a medium bowl, stir together the broccoli, carrots, garlic, lemon zest, salt, mustard powder, broth, and coconut oil.
3. Evenly spread the mixture into a baking pan. Cover with aluminum foil and place in the preheated oven. Bake for 30 minutes, stirring once.
4. Serve immediately.

Per Serving (2 Cups)
calories: 271 | fat: 15.1g | protein: 11.5g
carbs: 28.2g | fiber: 5.2g

Swiss Chard Spelt Pasta

Prep time: 5 minutes | Cook time: 5 minutes | Serves 2

1 head of Swiss chard, cut into ½-inch pieces	1 key lime, juiced, zested
1 cup spelt pasta, cooked	¼ teaspoon salt
2 green onions, sliced	¼ teaspoon cayenne pepper
¼ cup cilantro	1 tablespoon olive oil

1. Take a large skillet pan, place it over medium heat, add oil and when hot, add chard pieces and then cook for 4 minutes or more until wilted.
2. Remove pan from heat, transfer chards to a large bowl, add remaining ingredients and then toss until combined.
3. Serve straight away.

Per Serving
calories: 225 | fat: 7.1g | protein: 7.2g
carbs: 32.9g | fiber: 2.1g

Baked Butternut Squash and Apple

Prep time: 10 minutes | Cook time: 35 minutes | Serves 2

1½ pounds (680 g) butternut squash, peeled, deseeded, cut into chunks	2 tablespoons agave syrup
2 apples, cored, cut into ½-inch pieces	½ teaspoon sea salt
	2 tablespoons grapeseed oil

1. Switch on the oven, then set it to 375ºF (190ºC) and let it preheat.
2. Meanwhile, take a baking sheet and then spread squash pieces on it.
3. Take a small bowl, pour in oil, stir in salt and allspice until mixed, and then drizzle over squash pieces.

4. Cover the pan with foil and then bake for 20 minutes.
5. Meanwhile, place apple pieces in a medium bowl, drizzle with agave syrup, and then toss until coated.
6. When squash has baked, unwrap the baking sheet, spoon into the bowl containing apple and then stir until mixed.
7. Spread apple-squash mixture evenly on the baking sheet and then continue baking for 15 minutes.
8. Serve straight away.

Per Serving
calories: 127 | fat: 4.9g | protein: 1.1g
carbs: 22.3g | fiber: 5.2g

Ritzy Vegetable and Fruit Roast

Prep time: 15 minutes | Cook time: 60 minutes | Serves 4

1 butternut squash, peeled and cubed	peeled, cored, and sliced
1 baking pumpkin, peeled and cubed	3 fresh sage leaves, finely chopped
2 large carrots, peeled and cubed	1 teaspoon sea salt
2 green apples,	2 teaspoons coconut oil

1. Preheat the oven to 350ºF (180ºC).
2. In a large bowl, combine the butternut squash, pumpkin, carrots, apples, sage, salt, and coconut oil. Toss to coat evenly in the oil and seasonings. Transfer the vegetables to a roasting pan, in a single layer.
3. Roast for 60 minutes, stirring occasionally. Serve.

Per Serving (1 Cup)
calories: 177 | fat: 12.5g | protein: 4.2g
carbs: 44.5g | fiber: 6.4g

Spaghetti Squash with Zucchini Pesto

Prep time: 20 minutes | Cook time: 50 minutes | Serves 2

1 spaghetti squash	onion
2 teaspoons avocado oil	2 tablespoons avocado oil
Sea salt	1 tablespoon freshly squeezed lemon juice
Freshly ground black pepper	1 tablespoon nutritional yeast
1 zucchini, peeled	2 garlic cloves
2 stalks kale, stemmed	½ teaspoon sea salt
½ cup raw cashews	
¼ cup chopped	

1. Preheat the oven to 350ºF (180ºC). Line a baking sheet with parchment paper.
2. Halve the spaghetti squash lengthwise, scoop out the seeds, rub the insides and outer rims of both halves with avocado oil, sprinkle with salt and pepper, and place on a baking sheet. Bake for 45 to 50 minutes, or until tender.
3. Meanwhile, in a food processor, process the zucchini, kale, cashews, onion, avocado oil, lemon juice, nutritional yeast, garlic, and salt until well blended. Adjust seasonings, if necessary.
4. Using a fork, scrape out the insides of the squash into long, pasta-like strands. Transfer to a medium bowl.
5. Add the pesto, and toss gently until well mixed. Transfer to 2 plates or bowls and enjoy.

Per Serving

calories: 485 | fat: 36.6g | protein: 10.9g carbs: 36.8g | fiber: 7.7g

Broccoli and Wild Rice Bowl

Prep time: 10 minutes | Cook time: 20 minutes | Serves 4

1 cup bite-size broccoli florets	cider vinegar
6 garlic cloves, peeled	¼ teaspoon garlic powder
1 teaspoon avocado oil	¼ to ½ teaspoon sea salt
Pinch sea salt	Pinch freshly ground black pepper
Pinch black pepper	1 cup cooked wild rice
Pinch garlic powder	¼ cup slivered almonds
6 roasted garlic cloves (from above)	2 tablespoons diced onion
1 cup raw cashews	½ cup chopped collard greens
1 cup water	
½ teaspoon avocado oil	
½ teaspoon apple	

1. Preheat the oven to 400ºF (205ºC). Line a baking sheet with parchment paper.
2. In a small bowl, toss the broccoli and garlic with the avocado oil to coat. Season with the salt, pepper, and garlic powder, and transfer to the prepared baking sheet.
3. Roast the broccoli and garlic for 15 to 20 minutes, or until the broccoli gets soft and slightly crispy.
4. In a high-speed blender, blend together the roasted garlic cloves, cashews, water, avocado oil, vinegar, garlic powder, salt, and pepper until creamy and smooth. Adjust the seasonings, if necessary.
5. In a serving bowl, stir together the cooked rice with the roasted broccoli, almond slivers, onion, and collard greens. Stir in the dressing and enjoy.

Per Serving

calories: 315 | fat: 21.2g | protein: 9.6g carbs: 26.1g | fiber: 3.4g

Lentil Burgers

Prep time: 15 minutes | Cook time: 30 minutes | Makes 4 burgers

½ cup dry lentils (equals 1 cup cooked)
½ cup almond flour
½ teaspoon sea salt
½ teaspoon freshly ground black pepper
½ cup diced onion
½ cup chopped

cilantro leaves
½ to 1 jalapeño, diced
2 garlic cloves, crushed
1 tablespoon coconut flour
1 tablespoon avocado oil

1. Prepare the dry lentils according to the package directions. Set aside to cool.
2. In a medium bowl, stir together the cooled lentils, almond flour, salt, pepper, onion, cilantro, jalapeño, and garlic until well combined.
3. In a food processor, process half of the lentil mixture until it reaches a paste-like consistency.
4. Return the processed lentil mixture to the bowl with the other half of the mixture, and stir until well combined. The mixture should be very moist, so mix in the coconut flour to help it hold together.
5. Take one-quarter of the mixture, squeeze it together in your hand, and flatten it with the palms into a small burger. Repeat to make 3 more patties with the remaining lentil mixture.
6. In a large skillet over medium-high heat, heat the avocado oil. Add the burgers; cook for 4 to 6 minutes on each side, or until they become golden, flipping them gently; and serve.

Per Serving (1 Burger)
calories: 186 | fat: 7.6g | protein: 6.3g
carbs: 24.0g | fiber: 4.7g

Bell Pepper Stuffed Mushrooms

Prep time: 10 minutes | Cook time: 20 minutes | Serves 2

2 large portobello mushrooms
Avocado oil, for rubbing
Sea salt
Freshly ground black pepper
½ red bell pepper, diced
½ orange bell pepper, diced
½ yellow bell

pepper, diced
¼ cup diced red onion
2 garlic cloves, crushed
2 teaspoons avocado oil
½ teaspoon sea salt
½ teaspoon freshly ground black pepper

1. Preheat the oven to 350ºF (180ºC). Line a baking sheet with parchment paper.
2. Quickly rinse and dry the mushrooms. Remove the stems, and using the tip of a spoon, scoop out the black gills. Rub the mushrooms all over with avocado oil, and sprinkle with salt and pepper.
3. Transfer the mushrooms to the prepared baking sheet, and bake for 15 to 20 minutes, or until the mushrooms are as soft as you like.
4. Meanwhile, in a small bowl, stir together the bell peppers, onion, garlic, avocado oil, salt, and pepper until well combined.
5. Remove the mushrooms from the oven, and discard any accumulated liquid.
6. Divide the stuffing mixture evenly between the 2 mushrooms and serve immediately.

Per Serving
calories: 219 | fat: 18.9g | protein: 2.5g
carbs: 12.4g | fiber: 2.0g

Tahini Beet Pizza

Prep time: 10 minutes | Cook time: 15 minutes | Makes 4 small pieces

For the Crust:
1¼ cup almond flour
3 tablespoons coconut oil
½ teaspoon sea salt
½ teaspoon garlic powder

For the Tahini-Beet Spread:
2 beets, peeled and cubed
1 tablespoon tahini
1 tablespoon avocado oil
1 tablespoon freshly squeezed lemon juice
2 garlic cloves
⅛ teaspoon sea salt
Pinch freshly ground black pepper

For Assembling:
Mushrooms, red onions, dandelion greens, asparagus, jalapeños, artichokes, arugula, broccoli, basil, dulse flakes (optional toppings)

1. Preheat the oven to 375ºF (190ºC). Line a baking sheet with parchment paper.
2. To Prepare the Crust
3. In a small bowl, stir together the almond flour, coconut oil, salt, and garlic powder until well combined.
4. Transfer to the prepared baking pan, and squeeze the mixture together until it forms a ball shape. Lay another sheet of parchment paper on top of the ball, and use a rolling pin to roll the dough out over the parchment paper into a 7-by-7-inch square.
5. Bake for about 14 minutes, until the edges turn golden brown.
6. To Prepare the Tahini-Beet Spread
7. Meanwhile, in a food processor, process the beets, tahini, avocado oil, lemon juice, garlic, salt, and pepper until thick and creamy. Adjust the seasonings, if necessary.
8. To Assemble
9. When the crust is ready, spread the tahini-beet spread evenly over it, top the pizza with the favorite alkaline veggies, cut into 4 slices, and enjoy.

Per Serving (1 Piece)
calories: 305 | fat: 16.2g | protein: 5.5g
carbs: 35.6g | fiber: 2.6g

Squash Pasta with Spaghetti Sauce

Prep time: 15 minutes | Cook time: 1 hour 5 minutes | Serves 2

2 cups spaghetti squash, spiralized
2 tablespoons plus 1 teaspoon coconut oil
¼ onion, chopped
2 teaspoons sea salt, divided
1 teaspoon minced garlic
½ teaspoon red pepper flakes
1 (6-ounce / 170-g) can tomato paste
1 (16-ounce / 454-g) jar spaghetti sauce
½ cup water

1. Preheat the oven to 350ºF (180ºC).
2. To roast a spaghetti squash, cut the squash in half lengthwise and scrape out the seeds. Brush each half with coconut oil and season with 1 teaspoon sea salt. Place the squash halves cut-side up on a baking sheet and roast in the preheated oven for about 50 minutes, or until fork tender.
3. In a medium pot set over medium heat, add the onion and coconut oil. Sauté for about 5 minutes, or until tender.
4. Add the remaining salt, garlic, red pepper flakes, and tomato paste. Stir until combined.
5. Add the spaghetti sauce and water. Simmer for 10 minutes.
6. Add the spaghetti squash and stir to combine.
7. Serve immediately.

Per Serving (2 Cups)
calories: 285 | fat: 3.7g | protein: 8.5g
carbs: 36.7g | fiber: 7.5g

Mango-Habanero Cauliflower Wraps

Prep time: 5 minutes | Cook time: 35 minutes | Makes 2 wraps

2 cups bite-size cauliflower florets
1 tablespoon avocado oil
¼ cup almond flour
¼ cup nutritional yeast
½ teaspoon garlic powder
¼ teaspoon sea salt
¼ teaspoon freshly ground black pepper
1 cup cubed mango
1 habanero pepper
2 garlic cloves
2 tablespoons apple cider vinegar
⅛ teaspoon sea salt
½ to 1 cup mixed salad greens
2 fresh collard green leaves

1. Preheat the oven to 350ºF (180ºC). Line a baking sheet with parchment paper.
2. In a medium bowl, toss the cauliflower with the avocado oil to coat.
3. In a small bowl, stir together the almond flour, nutritional yeast, garlic powder, salt, and pepper until well combined.
4. Add the breading mixture to the cauliflower, and toss until all pieces are covered. Transfer to the prepared baking sheet.
5. Roast the cauliflower for 30 to 35 minutes, or until soft.
6. Meanwhile, in a blender, blend together the mango, habanero, garlic, vinegar, and salt until well combined. (Take extra precautions when handling the habanero pepper: Use rubber gloves or wash your hands thoroughly after handling.)
7. Place half of the mixed salad greens in the center of a collard green leaf, top it with half of the cauliflower, drizzle the sauce on top, and wrap like a burrito. Repeat to make the second wrap, and enjoy.

Per Serving
calories: 296 | fat: 9.6g | protein: 13.5g
carbs: 46.2g | fiber: 11.3g

Broccoli-Basil Pesto Stuffed Sweet Potato

Prep time: 10 minutes | Cook time: 1 hour 15 minutes | Makes 2 potatoes

2 large sweet potatoes
2½ cups broccoli
2½ cups almonds
½ cup fresh basil leaves
¼ cup onion
2 garlic cloves
2 tablespoon avocado oil
¼ cup nutritional yeast
½ teaspoon sea salt

1. Preheat the oven to 350ºF (180ºC).
2. Pierce the sweet potatoes all over with a fork. Place the sweet potatoes on a baking sheet, and bake for 1 hour and 15 minutes, or until they are soft.
3. Meanwhile, prepare the pesto. In a food processor, pulse the broccoli, almonds, basil, onion, garlic, avocado oil, nutritional yeast, and salt until the broccoli and almonds are ground into tiny pieces. Adjust the seasonings, if necessary.
4. When the potatoes are ready, cut them in half lengthwise, and gently scoop out the insides of the potato, taking care not to tear the potato skin; add the baked potato filling to a medium bowl, and add the pesto mixture; gently stir together.
5. Divide the mixture in half, add each half back into the two empty potato skins, and serve.

Per Serving
calories: 1002 | fat: 73.6g | protein: 38.2g
carbs: 64.8g | fiber: 26.5g

Garbanzo and Mushroom "Sausage" Links

Prep time: 15minutes | Cook time: 5 minutes | Serves 8 to 10

2 cups cooked garbanzo beans
1 quartered Roma tomato
1 cup quartered mushrooms
½ cup chopped onion
½ cup garbanzo bean flour
1 tablespoon onion powder
1 teaspoon ground sage
1 teaspoon basil
1 teaspoon oregano
1 teaspoon dill
½ teaspoon ground cloves
1 teaspoon pure sea salt
½ teaspoon cayenne powder
2 tablespoons grape seed oil

1. Put all the ingredients, except the garbanzo bean flour and grape seed oil, into a food processor.
2. Blend for 15 seconds.
3. Add the garbanzo bean flour to the mixture and blend for 30 more seconds until well combined.
4. Put the mixture into a piping bag and cut a small piece from the bottom corner.
5. Add grape seed oil to a skillet and warm on high heat.
6. Reduce to medium heat. Squeeze out the prepared mixture into the pan to form sausages.
7. Cook them for about 3 to 4 minutes on all sides. Turn carefully to prevent them falling apart.
8. Serve and enjoy.

Per Serving
calories: 105 | fat: 4.0g | protein: 4.5g
carbs: 13.6g | fiber: 3.5g

Apple and Butternut Squash Burger

Prep time: 10 minutes | Cook time: 1 hour | Serves 2

¾ cup diced butternut squash
½ cup diced apples
1 cup cooked wild rice
¼ cup chopped shallots
½ tablespoon thyme
¼ teaspoon sea salt, divided
1 tablespoon pumpkin seeds, unsalted
1 tablespoon grapeseed oil
2 spelt burgers, halved, toasted

1. Switch on the oven, then set it to 400ºF (205ºC) and let it preheat.
2. Meanwhile, take a cookie sheet, line it with parchment sheet, spread squash pieces on it and then sprinkle with ⅛ teaspoon salt.
3. Bake the squash for 15 minutes, then add shallots and apple, sprinkle with remaining salt, and then bake for 20 to 30 minutes until cooked.
4. When done, let the vegetable mixture cool for 15 minutes, transfer it into a food processor, add thyme and then pulse until a chunky mixture comes together.
5. Add pumpkin seeds and cooked wild rice, pulse until combined, and then tip the mixture in a bowl.
6. Taste the mixture to adjust and then shape it into two patties.
7. Take a skillet pan, place it over medium heat, add oil and when hot, place patties in it and then cook for 5 to 7 minutes per side until browned.
8. Sandwich patties in burger buns and then serve.

Per Serving
calories: 251 | fat: 3.9g | protein: 5.8g
carbs: 50.9g | fiber: 5.1g

Ratatouille

Prep time: 15 minutes | Cook time: 35 minutes | Serves 4

Cooking spray
½ onion, chopped
2 garlic cloves, minced
1 (6-ounce / 170-g) can tomato paste
4 tablespoons coconut oil, divided
¾ cup water
½ teaspoon sea salt
1 small eggplant, thinly sliced
1 zucchini, thinly sliced
1 yellow squash, thinly sliced
1 red bell pepper, thinly sliced
1 yellow bell pepper, thinly sliced
2 large tomatoes, thinly sliced
1 teaspoon fresh thyme leaves

1. Preheat the oven to 375ºF (190ºC).
2. Spray a small skillet with cooking spray. Set the pan over medium heat, add the onion and garlic, and sauté for 5 minutes, or until soft. Remove from the heat and set aside.
3. In a small bowl, combine the tomato paste, onion mixture, 1 tablespoon coconut oil, and the water. Season with the salt. Spread this mixture along the bottom of a baking dish.
4. In a large bowl, add the eggplant, zucchini, yellow squash, red bell pepper, yellow bell pepper, tomatoes, tomatoes, and 1 tablespoon coconut oil. Toss to evenly coat all the vegetables.
5. Following the inside edge of the baking dish and working inward, top the tomato mixture with the vegetables, in layers and alternating by types (e.g., 1 slice of eggplant, then 1 zucchini slice, 1 squash slice, 1 red bell pepper slice, 1 yellow pepper slice, and finally, 1 tomato slice). Repeat the spiral layers until all vegetables are used.
6. Season with the thyme and finish by drizzling the remaining 2 tablespoons coconut oil over the vegetables. Cover with aluminum foil, or parchment paper, and place in the preheated oven.
7. Bake for about 30 minutes, or until the vegetables are tender and fully roasted.

Per Serving
calories: 206 | fat: 14.5g | protein: 3.5g
carbs: 19.0g | fiber: 7.8g

Hearty Vegetable Nori Rolls

Prep time: 10 minutes | Cook time: 0 minutes | Makes 2 large rolls

1 avocado, pitted and halved
¼ cup fresh cilantro leaves
2 tablespoons freshly squeezed lemon juice
½ to 1 jalapeño
¼ teaspoon sea salt
2 collard green leaves
2 nori sheets
½ red bell pepper, sliced
½ orange bell pepper, sliced
½ yellow bell pepper, sliced
½ cup chopped purple cabbage
2 tablespoons chopped fresh cilantro leaves

1. In a blender, blend together the avocado, cilantro, lemon juice, jalapeño, and salt until smooth.
2. Lay 1 collard green leaf flat, and place 1 nori sheet on top of it.
3. Spread half the avocado-jalapeño mixture down the center.
4. Take half of the bell peppers, cabbage, and cilantro, and arrange in the center of the nori sheet on the avocado-jalapeño spread. Roll like a burrito. Repeat with the remaining collard green leaf, nori, bell pepper, cabbage, and cilantro.
5. Enjoy each roll whole or halved.

Per Serving (1 Roll)
calories: 207 | fat: 15.1g | protein: 3.7g
carbs: 19.3g | fiber: 8.9g

Curried Eggplant with Quinoa

Prep time: 5 minutes | Cook time: 35 minutes | Serves 2

1 eggplant, cooled, with contents removed from the shell and reserved
Juice of 1 lemon
1 teaspoon sea salt

1 teaspoon sesame oil
1 teaspoon curry powder
Water, as needed
Cooked quinoa, for serving

1. Preheat the oven to 300°F.
2. To roast eggplant, simply slice it, add a little sea salt, and bake in the preheated oven for about 30 minutes, or until it's soft.
3. In a food processor, combine the eggplant, lemon juice, salt, sesame oil, and curry powder. Blend until smooth.
4. To a small saucepan set over medium heat, transfer the eggplant mixture and warm it for about 5 minutes. Add some water to thin, if necessary.
5. Serve over quinoa.

Per Serving
calories: 82 | fat: 2.7g | protein: 2.3g | carbs: 14.2g | fiber: 8.5g

Coconut Brussels Sprouts

Prep time: 5 minutes | Cook time: 10 minutes | Serves 2

½ cup light unsweetened coconut milk
1 teaspoon freshly squeezed lime juice
1½ teaspoons ground ginger
½ teaspoon chili-garlic sauce
1 packet stevia

¾ pound (340 g) Brussels sprouts, ends removed, trimmed, and halved
1 tablespoon coconut oil
½ teaspoon sea salt

1. In a medium saucepan set over medium heat, combine the coconut milk, lime juice, ground ginger, chili-garlic sauce, and stevia. Bring ingredients to a simmer. Cook for 5 minutes. Remove from the heat and set aside.
2. Preheat the broiler.
3. In a medium bowl, add the Brussels sprouts, coconut oil, and sea salt. Toss to combine.
4. Transfer to a medium cast-iron pan or ovenproof skillet. Sauté over medium heat for 5 minutes.
5. Place the skillet under the broiler and broil for 3 minutes, or until the leaves are slightly browned.
6. Transfer the Brussels sprouts to a medium bowl. Add the sauce and toss to coat. Serve immediately.

Per Serving
calories: 170 | fat: 8.6g | protein: 7.8g | carbs: 19.5g | fiber: 6.6g

Avocado and Sprout Lettuce Wraps

Prep time: 10 minutes | Cook time: 0 minutes | Serves 2

½ cup cherry tomatoes, halved
1 avocado, peeled, pitted, sliced
½ cup sprouts
½ of medium white onion, peeled, sliced
2 large lettuce leaves

2 tablespoons key lime juice
½ tablespoon raisins
¼ teaspoon salt
⅛ teaspoon cayenne pepper

1. Take a small bowl, add lime juice, add salt and pepper and then stir until mixed.
2. Take a medium bowl, place all the vegetables in it except for lettuce, drizzle with the lime juice mixture and then toss until mixed.
3. Place a lettuce leaves on a plate, top with half of the vegetable mixture, and then roll it tightly.
4. Repeat with the other lettuce wrap and then serve.

Per Serving
calories: 156 | fat: 10.6g | protein: 4.9g | carbs: 13.3g | fiber: 3.4g

Veg and Quinoa Stuffed Bell Peppers

Prep time: 5 minutes | Cook time: 20 minutes | Serves 2

Cooking spray
1 teaspoon coconut oil
½ cup chopped vegetables, zucchini, carrots, or broccoli
1 cup cooked quinoa

1 teaspoon garlic powder
1 teaspoon onion powder
1 teaspoon sea salt
2 bell peppers, any color, cored and seeded; tops removed and reserved

1. Preheat the oven to 350ºF (180ºC).
2. Coat a baking pan with cooking spray.
3. In a medium saucepan set over medium heat, add the coconut oil and chopped vegetables. Sauté for 5 minutes, or until softened.
4. Add the quinoa, garlic powder, onion powder, and salt. Stir to combine.
5. Place each bell pepper upright in the prepared pan. Fill each pepper with one-half of the quinoa-vegetable mix. Top each pepper with its reserved top.
6. Cover with aluminum foil, place in the preheated oven, and bake for 15 minutes, or until the peppers are soft.

Per Serving (1 Pepper)
calories: 215 | fat: 5.2g | protein: 7.1g | carbs: 34.7g | fiber: 5.4g

Basil Cashew and Artichoke Lentil Pasta

Prep time: 5 minutes | Cook time: 10 minutes | Serves 2 to 4

2 cups red lentil pasta
1¼ cups raw cashews
¾ cup almond milk
1 tablespoon freshly squeezed lemon juice
3 garlic cloves
1 tablespoon nutritional yeast

1 tablespoon avocado oil
½ teaspoon sea salt
¼ teaspoon freshly ground black pepper
1 can artichoke hearts, chopped
1 bunch fresh basil, cut into long strips (about 1 cup)

1. Cook the pasta according the package directions.
2. Meanwhile, prepare the sauce. In a high-speed blender, blend together the cashews, almond milk, lemon juice, garlic, nutritional yeast, avocado oil, salt, and pepper until creamy and smooth.
3. Transfer the drained pasta to a large bowl with the sauce, artichokes, and basil. Toss gently until well mixed, transfer to 2 large or 4 small plates, and enjoy.

Per Serving
calories: 450 | fat: 24.9g | protein: 13.5g | carbs: 50.7g | fiber: 11.2g

Artichoke Sweet Potato Slices

Prep time: 5 minutes | Cook time: 45 minutes | Makes 8 pieces

2 unpeeled sweet potatoes, cut into 4 (¼-inch-thick) lengthwise slices
1 red bell pepper, quartered
6 teaspoons avocado oil, divided
½ teaspoon salt, plus 1 pinch

¼ teaspoon freshly ground black pepper, plus 1 pinch
1 (14-ounce / 397-g) can artichoke hearts
2 garlic cloves

1. Preheat the oven to 350ºF (180ºC). Line a baking sheet with parchment paper.
2. Transfer the sweet potato and bell pepper to the prepared baking sheet, and drizzle with 2 teaspoons avocado oil, the pinch salt, and the pinch pepper.
3. Bake for 30 minutes. Flip them over and return to the oven for an additional 15 minutes.
4. In a food processor, pulse the roasted red bell pepper, the remaining 4 teaspoons avocado oil, the remaining ½ teaspoon salt, the remaining ¼ teaspoon black pepper, the artichoke hearts, and the garlic until well combined but still chunky. Adjust seasonings, if necessary.
5. Top the sweet potato slices with the spread and enjoy.

Per Serving (1 Piece)
calories: 87 | fat: 3.5g | protein: 2.3g | carbs: 13.0g | fiber: 4.0g

Zucchini Bacon

Prep time: 10 minutes | Cook time: 20 minutes | Serves 2

2 zucchini, cut into strips
1 tablespoon onion powder
1 tablespoon sea salt
½ teaspoon cayenne powder
¼ cup date sugar

2 tablespoons agave syrup
1 teaspoon liquid smoke
¼ cup spring water
1 tablespoon grapeseed oil

1. Take a medium saucepan, place it over medium heat, add all the ingredients except for zucchini and oil and then cook until sugar has dissolved.
2. Then place zucchini strips in a large bowl, pour in the mixture from the saucepan, toss until coated, and then let it marinate for a minimum of 1 hour.
3. When ready to cook, switch on the oven, set it to 400ºF (205ºC), and let it preheat.
4. Take a baking sheet, line it with parchment sheet, grease with oil, arrange marinated zucchini strips on it, and then bake for 10 minutes.
5. Then flip the zucchini, continue cooking for 4 minutes and then let cool completely.
6. Serve straight away.

Per Serving
calories: 185 | fat: 2.1g | protein: 12.1g | carbs: 26.2g | fiber: 1.9g

Bell Pepper Mushroom Steak

Prep time: 10 minutes | Cook time: 10 minutes | Serves 2

2 portabella mushroom caps, ⅛-inch thick sliced
½ cup sliced green bell peppers
½ cup sliced white onions
½ cup sliced red bell peppers
¼ cup alkaline sauce

½ teaspoon sea salt
½ tablespoon onion powder
½ teaspoon dried oregano
½ teaspoon dried thyme
½ tablespoon grapeseed oil
2 spelt flatbread, toasted

1. Take a medium bowl, place sauce in it, add all the seasoning, and then whisk until combined.
2. Add mushroom slices, toss until coated, and then let them marinate for a minimum of 30 minutes, tossing halfway.
3. Then take a pan, place it over medium-high heat, add oil and when hot, add onion and pepper and cook for 3 to 5 minutes until tender-crisp.
4. Add mushroom slices, stir until mixed and continue cooking for 5 minutes.
5. Distribute vegetables evenly between flatbread, roll them, and then serve.

Per Serving
calories: 303 | fat: 18.1g | protein: 2.1g | carbs: 26.8g | fiber: 3.1g

Eggplant and Bell Pepper Stir-Fry

Prep time: 10 minutes | Cook time: 5 minutes | Serves 2 to 4

3 tablespoons avocado oil
3 cups cubed eggplant (about three-quarters of an eggplant)
2 tablespoons coconut aminos
2 garlic cloves, crushed
½ teaspoon sea salt

½ teaspoon freshly ground black pepper
½ orange bell pepper, diced
½ yellow bell pepper, diced
½ red bell pepper, diced
Chopped scallions and/or sesame seeds, for garnish (optional)

1. In a large skillet over medium-high heat, heat the avocado oil. Add the eggplant, coconut aminos, garlic, salt, and pepper, and sauté for 3 to 5 minutes, or until the eggplant is soft.
2. Reduce the heat to low, add the bell peppers, and toss just long enough for everything to be coated.
3. Remove from the heat, transfer to 2 large or 4 small plates, and serve garnished with scallions and/or sesame seeds (if using).

Per Serving
calories: 133 | fat: 10.8g | protein: 2.3g | carbs: 8.6g | fiber: 2.6g

Mushroom and Bell Pepper Fritters

Prep time: 10 minutes | Cook time: 10 minutes | Serves 2

1 cup chickpea flour
7 ounces (198 g) mushrooms, chopped
1 medium green bell pepper, cored, chopped
1 tablespoon onion powder
2 medium white onions, peeled, chopped

1 teaspoon sea salt
1 tablespoon oregano
⅛ teaspoon cayenne pepper
1 tablespoon grapeseed oil
1 tablespoon basil leaves, chopped
½ cup spring water

1. Take a large bowl, place all the vegetables in it, add all the seasonings, basil and oregano, stir until mixed, and then let the mixture rest for 5 minutes.
2. Add chickpea flour, stir until mixed and then stir in water until well combined and smooth.
3. Take a large skillet pan, place it over medium heat, add oil and when hot, ladle vegetable mixture in it in portions, press down each portion, and then cook for 3 to 4 minutes per side until cooked and golden brown.
4. Serve straight away.

Per Serving
calories: 282 | fat: 15.3g | protein: 13.9g | carbs: 26.1g | fiber: 4.9g

Mushroom and Kale Ravioli

Prep time: 25 minutes | Cook time: 10 minutes | Serves 5

Filling:

1 cup chickpea flour
1 quartered Roma tomato
2 cups quartered mushrooms
1 cup chopped kale
$1/3$ cup diced onions
1 cup diced green and red bell peppers
1 tablespoon onion powder

1 teaspoon ginger
2 teaspoons oregano
2 teaspoons dill
2 teaspoons basil
2 teaspoons thyme
1 teaspoon pure sea salt
½ teaspoon cayenne

Dough:

½ cup chickpea flour
1½ cups spelt flour
½ teaspoon oregano

½ teaspoon basil
1 teaspoon pure sea salt
¾ cup spring water

Cheese:

½ cup soaked Brazil nuts (overnight or for at least 3 hours)
2 teaspoons onion powder
½ teaspoon oregano

1 teaspoon pure sea salt
½ teaspoon cayenne powder
½ cup spring water

1. Blend all filling ingredients, except the chickpea flour, in a food processor for 30 to 40 seconds.
2. Add chickpea flour to the mixture and blend until well combined.
3. Add grape seed oil to a skillet and warm on high heat.
4. Reduce to medium heat. Spread out the ravioli filling to the skillet and cook for 3 to 4 minutes on all sides.
5. Break up the filling and cook for 3 more minutes, then transfer it to a medium bowl.
6. Add all ingredients for the cheese to the food processor and blend until consistency is creamy. If it's too thick, add some spring water.
7. Mix the filling with the cheese mixture in the bowl.
8. Put all the dry ingredients for the dough in the food processor and blend for 10 to 20 seconds. Slowly add spring water while blending until dough can be shaped into a ball.
9. Spread flour on the working space. Take ¼ of the dough and roll it out into a thin sheet.
10. Place rounded teaspoonfuls of filling and cheese 1 inch apart on one side of the dough. Fold the dough over and press together around the filling to seal. Cut it into individual ravioli with a pastry cutter or knife.
11. Repeat steps 9 and 10 with the remaining dough and filling.
12. Bring a pot of spring water to a boil. add a little pure sea salt and grape seed oil, then cook the ravioli for about 4 to 6 minutes.
13. Strain and serve.

Per Serving
calories: 365 | fat: 12.7g | protein: 14.2g | carbs: 51.0g | fiber: 7.2g

Chapter 6: Grains

Amaranth and Zucchini Patties

Prep time: 10 minutes | Cook time: 12 minutes | Serves 2

½ cup amaranth, cooked
½ of medium white onion, peeled, chopped
¼ cup grated zucchini
¼ cup chopped red bell pepper
$1/_3$ teaspoon salt
¼ teaspoon cayenne pepper
¼ teaspoon coriander powder
¼ teaspoon key lime zest
2 tablespoons grapeseed oil

1. Take a small frying pan, place it over medium heat, add 1 tablespoon oil and when hot, add onion and then cook for 5 minutes until tender.
2. Add zucchini and red pepper, stir until mixed and cook for 3 minutes.
3. Add remaining ingredients except for oil and amaranth, stir until mixed, then remove the pan from heat and cool for 10 minutes.
4. Take a medium bowl, place cooked amaranth in it, add vegetable mixture, stir until combined, and then shape the mixture into evenly sized patties.
5. Take a large skillet pan, place it over medium heat, add remaining oil and when hot, place patties in it and then cook for 3 minutes per side until golden brown.
6. Serve straight away.

Per Serving
calories: 147 | fat: 2.1g | protein: 10.1g
carbs: 23.8g | fiber: 7.9g

Amaranth, Zucchini, and Kale Patties

Prep time: 10 minutes | Cook time: 40 minutes | Serves 2

½ of medium white onion, peeled, minced
½ cup amaranth, cooked
1 medium zucchini, grated
¼ cup chopped basil
1½ cups kale, chopped
¼ cup chopped dill
2 tablespoons spelt flour
½ teaspoon salt
¼ teaspoon cayenne pepper
1 tablespoon olive oil
1½ tablespoon tahini
1 tablespoon key lime juice

1. Switch on the oven, then set it to 400ºF (205ºC) and let it preheat.
2. Meanwhile, take a skillet pan, place it over medium heat, add oil and when hot, add onion and cook for 5 minutes until tender.
3. Add zucchini, cook for 3 to 5 minutes until soft, then add kale and cook for 5 minutes until wilted.
4. Spoon the mixture into a bowl, add remaining ingredients, stir until mixed, and then shape the mixture into evenly sized patties.
5. Arrange patties onto a baking sheet and then bake for 15 minutes per side until golden brown and cooked.
6. Serve straight away.

Per Serving
calories: 153 | fat: 2.9g | protein: 7.1g
carbs: 28.9g | fiber: 6.1g

Mushroom and Onion Risotto

Prep time: 5 minutes | Cook time: 1 hour 25 minutes | Serves 2

4 ounces (113 g) sliced mushrooms	grapeseed oil
¼ of an onion, chopped	2 cups vegetable broth, homemade
1 cup wild rice	$1/3$ teaspoon salt
1 tablespoon	¼ teaspoon cayenne pepper

1. Take a medium pot, place it over medium heat add oil and when hot, add onion and mushroom and then cook for 4 to 5 minutes until mushrooms have turned golden brown and the liquid in the pan have evaporated.
2. Add rice, stir until mixed, cook for 1 minute, and then stir in salt and cayenne pepper.
3. Pour in the broth, switch heat to the low level and then cook the rice for 1 hour and 20 minutes until rice is tender.
4. Serve straight away.

Per Serving
calories: 135 | fat: 1.4g | protein: 4.6g carbs: 25.1g | fiber: 2.5g

Raisin Spelt Cookies

Prep time: 10 minutes | Cook time: 18 minutes | Serves 2

1 cup spelt flour	spring water
$1/3$ cup raisins	$1/16$ teaspoon sea salt
½ cup dates, pitted	2 tablespoons agave syrup
3½ tablespoons, applesauce homemade or puréed apples	1 ¾ tablespoon grapeseed oil
$2/3$ tablespoon	

1. Switch on the oven, then set it to 350ºF (180ºC) and let it preheat.

2. Meanwhile, place flour in a food processor, add dates and salt in it, and then pulse until well blended.
3. Transfer flour mixture into a medium bowl, add remaining ingredients, and then stir until well mixed.
4. Divide the mixture into parts, each part about 2 tablespoons the mixture, and then shape each part into a ball.
5. Place the cookie ball on a cookie sheet lined with parchment sheet, flatten it slightly by using a fork and then bake for 18 minutes until done.
6. Let cookies cool for 10 minutes and then serve.

Per Serving
calories: 149 | fat: 4.1g | protein: 3.2g carbs: 55.4g | fiber: 2.1g

Basil Quinoa Veg Bowl

Prep time: 5 minutes | Cook time: 3 minutes | Serves 2

$1/3$ cup quinoa, cooked	$1/3$ cup basil leaves
¼ cup cherry tomatoes, quartered	1 tablespoon grapeseed oil
½ of green bell pepper, chopped	¼ teaspoon salt
	$1/8$ teaspoon cayenne pepper

1. Take a pan, place it over medium heat, add oil and when hot, add cherry tomatoes and bell pepper and cook for 2 to 3 minutes until tender-crisp.
2. Take a medium bowl, place cooked quinoa in it, add tomatoes and bell pepper mixture, and then add basil leaves.
3. Season with salt and cayenne pepper, stir until mixed, and then serve.

Per Serving
calories: 142 | fat: 6.3g | protein: 6.6g carbs: 32.1g | fiber: 4.2g

Fried Rice with Mushroom and Zucchini

Prep time: 5 minutes | Cook time: 15 minutes | Serves 2

½ cup sliced mushrooms
1 cup cooked wild rice
½ cup sliced red bell pepper
¼ of a medium onion, peeled, cubed
½ cup sliced zucchini
½ teaspoon salt
¼ teaspoon cayenne pepper
1 tablespoon grapeseed oil

1. Take a medium skillet pan, place it over medium heat, add oil and when hot, add onion and cook for 5 minutes until browned.
2. Add remaining vegetables, stir until mixed, and then cook for 5 minutes until almost soft.
3. Add rice, stir until combined and cook for 3 minutes until golden brown.
4. Serve straight away.

Per Serving
calories: 141 | fat: 6.9g | protein: 3.8g
carbs: 14.9g | fiber: 1.2g

Blackberry Flavor Banana and Quinoa Bars

Prep time: 10 minutes | Cook time: 10 minutes | Serves 2

½ cup spelt flour
2 baby burro bananas
1 cup quinoa flakes
$1/16$ teaspoon sea salt
1 tablespoon agave nectar
¼ cup grapeseed oil
½ cup alkaline blackberry jam

1. Switch on the oven, then set it to 350ºF (180ºC) and let it preheat.
2. Meanwhile, place peeled burro bananas in a medium bowl and then mash by using a fork.
3. Add agave nectar and oil, stir until well combined, and then stir in salt, flour, and quinoa flakes until a sticky dough comes together.
4. Take a square dish, line it with parchment sheet, spread two-third of the prepared dough in its bottom, layer with blackberry jam, and then top with remaining dough.
5. Bake for 10 minutes and then let the dough cool for 15 minutes.
6. Cut the dough into 4 bars and then serve.

Per Serving
calories: 109 | fat: 3.1g | protein: 1.5g
carbs: 19.3g | fiber: 1.5g

Date and Kamut Porridge

Prep time: 5 minutes | Cook time: 15 minutes | Serves 2

1 cup dates, pitted, chopped
1 cup rolled kamut
flakes
⅛ teaspoon salt
2 cups spring water

1. Place kamut flakes in a small saucepan, pour in the water, and let soak for overnight.
2. Then stir in salt, place the pan over medium-high heat and bring the mixture to a slow boil.
3. Switch heat to medium-low level and then continue cooking for 10 minutes or more until all the liquid has absorbed.
4. Remove pan from heat, add dates into the porridge and then stir until mixed.
5. Divide porridge between two bowls, drizzle with agave syrup if needed, and then serve.

Per Serving
calories: 133 | fat: 0.9g | protein: 0.2g
carbs: 30.3g | fiber: 1.9g

Amaranth and Quinoa Porridge

Prep time: 5 minutes | Cook time: 15 minutes | Serves 2

½ cup amaranth, cooked
2 tablespoons agave syrup
½ cup black quinoa,
cooked
½ cup soft-jelly coconut milk
2 cups spring water

1. Take a medium saucepan, place it over medium heat, add cooked quinoa and amaranth, pour in the water, stir until mixed, and then bring it a boil.
2. Switch heat to the low level and then simmer for 10 to 25 minutes until grains have absorbed all the liquid.
3. Pour in the milk, add agave syrup, stir until mixed, and then simmer for another 5 minutes until thoroughly cooked and slightly thickened.
4. Serve straight away.

Per Serving
calories: 205 | fat: 3.9g | protein: 8.1g
carbs: 32.8g | fiber: 2.9g

Amaranth and Walnut Milk Polenta

Prep time: 5 minutes | Cook time: 15 minutes | Serves 2

¾ cup amaranth
¼ teaspoon onion powder
¼ teaspoon salt
6 tablespoons walnut milk,
homemade
1½ cups vegetable broth, homemade
⅛ teaspoon cayenne pepper

1. Take a medium pot, place it over medium heat, pour in the broth, stir in salt and then bring it to a boil.
2. Then switch heat to medium-low level, whisk in amaranth and then cook for 10 to 20 minutes until slightly thick mixture comes together.

3. Add remaining ingredients, stir until mixed and continue cooking for 5 minutes.
4. Serve polenta with chickpeas.

Per Serving
calories: 173 | fat: 7.2g | protein: 4.4g
carbs: 18.6g | fiber: 1.7g

Quinoa and Chickpea Burgers

Prep time: 10 minutes | Cook time: 20 minutes | Serves 2

2 tablespoons chopped onion
¾ cup chickpeas
¼ cup cooked quinoa
1 tablespoon spring
water
1 tablespoon grapeseed oil
⅓ teaspoon salt
¼ teaspoon cayenne pepper

1. Switch on the oven, then set it to 375ºF (190ºC) and let it preheat.
2. Meanwhile, place onion, chickpeas, quinoa into a food processor and then pulse little chunky mixture comes together.
3. Add water, salt, and cayenne pepper and then pulse until the dough comes together.
4. Then tip the mixture into a medium bowl, cover it with its lid and then let it rest in the refrigerator for 15 minutes.
5. Shape the mixture into two patties, place them on a baking sheet lined with parchment paper and then bake for 20 minutes, turning halfway.
6. Then switch on the broiler and continue cooking for 2 minutes per side until golden brown.
7. You can serve the patties with spelt flour burgers and tahini butter.

Per Serving
calories: 315 | fat: 9.5g | protein: 10.2g
carbs: 47.8g | fiber: 5.9g

Oat and Walnut Milk Spelt Bread

Prep time: 10 minutes | Cook time: 40 minutes | Serves 2

1½ cups and 2 tablespoons spelt flour
¼ cup quick-cooking rolled oats
2 tablespoons sesame seeds
½ teaspoon sea salt

1 cup walnut milk, homemade, warmed
1 tablespoon agave syrup
1 tablespoon olive oil

1. Switch on the oven, then set it to 350ºF (180ºC), and let it preheat.
2. Meanwhile, take a medium bowl, place flour in it, add oats, salt, and sesame seeds and then stir until mixed.
3. Take a separate bowl, pour in milk, whisk in oil and agave syrup until combined, and then whisk in flour mixture until smooth.
4. Pour the batter into a loaf lined with parchment paper, sprinkle some more oats on top, pressing them into the batter, and then bake for 30 to 40 minutes until firm.
5. When done, let the bread cool completely on the wire rack, then cut it into slices and serve.

Per Serving
calories: 216 | fat: 4.9g | protein: 3.1g
carbs: 38.9g | fiber: 8.9g

Amaranth and Walnut Porridge

Prep time: 5 minutes | Cook time: 30 minutes | Serves 2

1 cup amaranth, soaked
2 tablespoons chopped walnuts
1 cup soft-jelly

coconut milk
1 cup spring water
Pinch salt
2 tablespoons agave syrup

1. Drain soaked amaranth, place them in a medium pot, pour in milk and water.
2. Place the pot over medium-high heat, bring the mixture to boil, then switch heat to medium level and cook for 25 minutes or more until amaranth has cooked.
3. Stir in salt and agave syrup, remove the pan from heat and distribute between two bowls.
4. Top amaranth with nuts and then serve.

Per Serving
calories: 374 | fat: 8.9g | protein: 13.9g
carbs: 64.1g | fiber: 14.1g

Hemp Seed Mayo Chickpea with Nori

Prep time: 10 minutes | Cook time: 0 minutes | Serves 2

¼ cup diced red onion
2 cups cooked chickpeas
⅛ cup diced green bell pepper
¼ teaspoon sea salt
2 teaspoons onion powder

¼ teaspoon salt
⅛ teaspoon cayenne pepper
⅔ cup alkaline hemp seed mayo
1 teaspoon dill
½ nori sheet, cut into small pieces

1. Take a large bowl, place chickpeas in it, and then mash them by using a fork.
2. Add remaining ingredients, stir until well mixed and then chill the salad for a minimum of 30 minutes.
3. Serve straight away.

Per Serving
calories: 260 | fat: 13.6g | protein: 6.2g
carbs: 27.8g | fiber: 5.1g

Chopped Walnuts with Amaranth

Prep time: 10 minutes | Cook time: 30 minutes | Serves 2

1 cup amaranth	chopped walnuts
2 cups spring water	2 tablespoons
¼ teaspoon salt	agave syrup
2 tablespoons	

1. Take a mediums saucepan, place it over medium-high heat, add amaranth, pour in water, and then bring it to a boil.
2. Then switch heat to medium level, cook it for 25 minutes until all the liquid has been absorbed, and then stir in salt.
3. Remove pan from heat, let amaranth rest for 10 minutes, and divide evenly between two bowls and then top with nuts and agave syrup.
4. Serve straight away.

Per Serving
calories: 176 | fat: 0g | protein: 1.4g carbs: 42.1g | fiber: 3.9g

Basil Teff Grain Sausage .

Prep time: 10 minutes | Cook time: 6 minutes | Serves 2

2 tablespoons diced onions	1 teaspoon basil
¾ cup cooked teff grain	1 teaspoon oregano
2 tablespoons diced red bell pepper	½ teaspoon sea salt
¼ cup chickpea flour	¼ teaspoon crushed red pepper
	1 tablespoon grapeseed oil

1. Take a medium skillet pan, place it over medium-high heat, add oil and when hot, add onion and peppers, and then cook for 2 to 3 minutes until tender.

2. Stir in chickpea flour, transfer the mixture into a medium bowl, add remaining ingredients, stir until well mixed, and then shape the mixture into evenly sized patties.
3. Return skillet pan over medium heat and when hot, place patties on it and then cook for 3 minutes per side until crisp and cooked.
4. Serve straight away.

Per Serving
calories: 88 | fat: 2.4g | protein: 4.5g carbs: 12.6g | fiber: 1.5g

Burro Banana Walnut Pancakes

Prep time: 10 minutes | Cook time: 6 minutes | Serves 2

½ cup spelt flour	sugar
¼ cup mashed burro banana	1½ teaspoons key lime juice
¼ cup and 2 tablespoons walnut milk, homemade	1 tablespoon grapeseed oil
½ teaspoon date	1½ teaspoon walnut butter, homemade

1. Take a medium bowl, pour in milk, stir in lime juice, let it rest for 5 minutes and then whisk in butter and mashed burro banana until combined.
2. Take a separate medium bowl, place flour in it, stir in sugar and then whisk in milk mixture until smooth.
3. Take a large skillet pan, place it over medium-high heat, add oil, and when hot, ladle the batter in it in 4 portions, shape each portion into a pancake and then cook for 2 to 3 minutes per side until golden brown and cooked.
4. Serve straight away.

Per Serving
calories: 104 | fat: 1.5g | protein: 6.8g carbs: 23.2g | fiber: 3.6g

Teff Grain Chickpea Burger

Prep time: 10 minutes | Cook time: 8 minutes | Serves 2

¾ cup cooked teff grains
¾ cup chickpea flour
2 tablespoons diced onion
2 tablespoons diced red bell pepper
½ teaspoon dill
¼ teaspoon salt
½ teaspoon oregano
⅛ teaspoon cayenne pepper
½ teaspoon basil
1 tablespoon grapeseed oil

1. Take a medium skillet pan, place it over medium heat, add oil and when hot, add onion and bell pepper and cook for 3 minutes until tender.
2. Transfer vegetables into the large bowl, add remaining ingredients, stir until mixed, and then shape the mixture into patties.
3. Place patties into the pan and then cook for 3 minutes per side until crisp and golden brown on all sides.
4. Serve straight away.

Per Serving
calories: 123 | fat: 4.3g | protein: 4.1g
carbs: 16.5g | fiber: 2.5g

Kamut Walnut Porridge

Prep time: 5 minutes | Cook time: 10 minutes | Serves 2

½ cup kamut
¼ teaspoon salt
2 tablespoons agave syrup
½ tablespoon coconut oil
2 cups walnut milk, homemade

1. Plug in a high-speed food processor or blender, add kamut in its jar, and then pulse until cracked.
2. Take a medium saucepan, add kamut in it along with salt, pour in the milk and then stir until combined.

3. Place the pan over high heat, bring the mixture to boil, then switch heat to medium-low level and simmer for 5 to 10 minutes until thickened to the desired level.
4. Then remove the pan from heat, stir agave syrup and oil into the porridge and then distribute evenly between two bowls.
5. Garnish the porridge with Dr. Sebi Diet's approved fruits and then serve.

Per Serving
calories: 184 | fat: 2.1g | protein: 10.1g
carbs: 29.9g | fiber: 4.1g

Walnut Spelt Biscuits

Prep time: 10 minutes | Cook time: 15 minutes | Serves 2

1 cup spelt flour
½ teaspoon salt
½ tablespoon baking powder
3 tablespoons
walnut butter, homemade
6 tablespoons walnut milk, homemade

1. Switch on the oven, then set it to 450ºF (235ºC) and let it preheat.
2. Meanwhile, place flour in a food processor, add salt, baking powder, and butter and then pulse until mixture resembles crumbs.
3. Tip the mixture in a bowl, stir in milk until dough comes together, and then roll it into 1-inch thick dough.
4. Use a cutter to cut out biscuits, arrange them on a baking sheet and then bake for 12 to 15 minutes until golden brown.
5. Serve straight away.

Per Serving
calories: 241 | fat: 3.9g | protein: 10.2g
carbs: 56.1g | fiber: 15.9g

Butternut Squash and Amaranth Bowl

Prep time: 5 minutes | Cook time: 10 minutes | Serves 2

10 ounces (283 g) cooked butter squash chunks
1 apple, peeled, cored, sliced
8 ounces (227 g) collard greens
1 teaspoon garam masala

1½ cup cooked amaranth
½ teaspoon salt
¼ teaspoon cayenne pepper
1 teaspoon and 1 tablespoon grapeseed oil

1. Take a pan, place it over medium heat, add 1 teaspoon oil and when hot, add squash piece, sprinkle with garam masala and ¼ teaspoon salt, stir until mixed and then cook for 5 minutes until hot.
2. Transfer squash mixture to a bowl, return skillet over medium heat, add remaining oil and when hot, add collard green, season with remaining salt, and then cook for 5 minutes until hot.
3. Divide amaranth between two bowls, top with apple, collards, and squash mixture and then serve.

Per Serving
calories: 326 | fat: 12.1g | protein: 9.3g | carbs: 49.9g | fiber: 8.2g

Chickpea Veg Hot Dogs

Prep time: 5 minutes | Cook time: 10 minutes | Serves 2

1 cup cooked chickpeas
1/3 cup diced green bell pepper,
1 cup spelt flour
1/3 cup diced white onion,
1 teaspoon coriander
¼ cup diced shallots,

1 tablespoon onion powder
2 teaspoons sea salt
½ teaspoon dill
1 tablespoon grapeseed oil
½ cup liquid from chickpeas

1. Take a pan, place it over medium heat, add oil and when hot, add chickpeas and all the vegetables and then cook for 5 minutes.
2. Transfer the chickpeas and vegetables in a food processor, add remaining ingredients and pulse until well combined.
3. Shape the mixture into hot dog shape rolls, and then wrap each hot dog in a parchment paper.
4. Boil some water in a pot, place a steamer on it, arrange wrapped hot dogs on it and then steam for 30 minutes.
5. When done, uncover the hot dogs and then fry for 10 minutes over medium heat until browned on all sides.
6. Serve hot dogs in spelt buns.

Per Serving
calories: 121 | fat: 2.1g | protein: 15.9g | carbs: 8.1g | fiber: 2.2g

Banana Muffin with Walnuts

Prep time: 10 minutes | Cook time: 20 minutes | Serves 2

1 burro banana, peeled, mashed
¾ cup spelt flour
½ burro banana, peeled, cut into chunks
6 tablespoons date sugar
6 tablespoons walnut milk, homemade

¼ teaspoon sea salt
½ tablespoon key lime juice
2 tablespoons grapeseed oil
¼ cup chopped walnuts

1. Switch on the oven, then set it to 400ºF (205ºC) and let it preheat.
2. Meanwhile, take a medium bowl, place all the dry ingredients in it and then stir until mixed.
3. Then a separate bowl, place the mashed burro banana in it, add all the wet ingredients, whisk until combined, and then whisk in flour mixture until smooth.
4. Fold in nuts and burro banana pieces and then spoon the mixture evenly into 4 muffin cups.
5. Bake the muffins for 15 to 20 minutes until firm and cooked and then serve.

Per Serving
calories: 205 | fat: 8.6g | protein: 3.2g | carbs: 30.1g | fiber: 1.5g

Blueberry, Banana, and Amaranth Pancakes

Prep time: 10 minutes | Cook time: 6 minutes | Serves 2

½ cup chickpea flour
¼ cup blueberries
1 burro banana, peeled
½ cup amaranth greens
½ cup spring water

½ teaspoon sea salt
1 tablespoon agave syrup
1 tablespoon walnut butter
1 tablespoon grapeseed oil

1. Plug in a high-speed food processor or blender and add all the ingredients in its jar.
2. Cover the blender jar with its lid, pulse for 40 to 60 seconds until smooth, tip the mixture in a bowl and let it rest for 10 minutes.
3. When ready to cook, take a large frying pan, place it over medium-high heat, add oil and then let it heat.
4. Scoop prepared batter into the hot pan into six portions, shape each portion like a pancake and then cook for 2 to 3 minutes per side until edges have cooked and firm.
5. Serve straight away.

Per Serving
calories: 145 | fat: 0.7g | protein: 5.9g | carbs: 31.5g | fiber: 5.5g

Authentic Falafel

Prep time: 10 minutes | Cook time: 10 minutes | Serves 2

2 cups cooked chickpeas
½ cup chopped white onion
½ cup chickpea flour
¼ cup green onions, chopped
1 teaspoon chopped basil
1 teaspoon chopped oregano
1 teaspoon onion powder

½ teaspoon of sea salt
½ teaspoon cayenne pepper
¹/₃ cup water from cooked chickpeas
1 tablespoon lime juice
1 tablespoon tahini
1 tablespoon grapeseed oil

1. Add chickpeas into a food processor, add remaining ingredients except for oil and then pulse until well blended.
2. Tip the mixture into a bowl and then shape into even size patties.
3. Take a large skillet pan, place it over medium heat, add oil and when hot, place prepared falafel patties in it and then cook for 4 to 5 minutes per side until golden brown and cooked.
4. Serve straight away.

Per Serving
calories: 183 | fat: 10.1g | protein: 5.9g | carbs: 18.1g | fiber: 4.1g

Vegetable Chickpea Quiche

Prep time: 10 minutes | Cook time: 15 minutes | Serves 2

For the Batter:
1½ tablespoon olive oil
1¼ cup chickpea flour
For the Filling:
½ cup chopped and cooked vegetables
½ teaspoon dried basil

1½cup spring water
1 teaspoon sea salt

½ teaspoon dried oregano

1. Switch on the oven, then set it to 500ºF (260ºC) and let it preheat.
2. Meanwhile, prepare the batter and for this, take a medium bowl, place all of its ingredients and then whisk until smooth batter comes together.
3. Add vegetables and herbs into the batter and then stir until combined.
4. Take six silicone muffin cups, grease them with oil, fill evenly with the prepared batter and then cook for 10 to 15 minutes until firm and turn golden brown.
5. Serve straight away.

Per Serving
calories: 183 | fat: 5.9g | protein: 7.9g | carbs: 25.4g | fiber: 7.1g

Herbed Rice Bowl

Prep time: 5 minutes | Cook time: 45 minutes | Serves 2

1 cup wild rice
½ teaspoon dried basil
½ teaspoon dried thyme

½ teaspoon dried oregano
3 cups vegetable broth, homemade
½ teaspoon salt

1. Take a medium saucepan, place it over medium-high heat, add rice, pour in water and bring it to a boil covering the pan with lid.
2. Then turn heat to the low level and simmer the rice for 40 minutes until tender.
3. Drain excess liquid from rice, add herbs, stir until mixed, and then serve.

Per Serving
calories: 166 | fat: 0.7g | protein: 6.6g | carbs: 35.1g | fiber: 2.9g

Mushroom and Pepper Chickpea Loaf

Prep time: 10 minutes | Cook time: 45 minutes | Serves 2

¼ cup spelt flour
1½ cups chickpeas, cooked
¾ cup diced onions
¼ cup minced basil
½ cup sliced white mushrooms
1 red bell pepper, cored, diced
1 tablespoon grapeseed oil
1 tablespoon and ¼ teaspoon granulated

onion, homemade
⅛ teaspoon dried thyme
½ teaspoon sea salt and more as needed
1/3 teaspoon dried sage
¼ teaspoon cayenne pepper and more as needed
¼ teaspoon dried oregano

1. Switch on the oven, then set it to 350ºF (180ºC) and let it preheat.
2. Meanwhile, take a large skillet pan, place it over medium-high heat, add oil in it and when hot, add onion, pepper, and mushroom and then cook for 3 minutes or until begin to tender.
3. Add minced basil into the pan, stir until mixed, remove the pan from heat, add all the seasonings and then stir until mixed.
4. Place chickpeas in a food processor, pulse until coarsely chopped, and then transfer into a medium bowl.
5. Add cooked vegetable mixture along with remaining ingredients, stir until well mixed and then spoon into a greased loaf pan.
6. Bake the loaf for 30 to 40 minutes until firm and cooked, cool it slightly, cut into slices and then serve.

Per Serving
calories: 269 | fat: 6.3g | protein: 10.4g | carbs: 46.1g | fiber: 9.5g

Spiced Chickpeas and Cherry Tomatoes

Prep time: 5 minutes | Cook time: 10 minutes | Serves 2

1½ cup cooked chickpeas
8 cherry tomatoes, chopped
1 medium onion, peeled, sliced
¾ cup vegetable broth, homemade
6 teaspoons spice mix

¼ teaspoon salt
½ tablespoon grapeseed oil
¼ teaspoon cayenne pepper
¾ cup tomato sauce, alkaline
6 tablespoons soft-jelly coconut milk

1. Take a large skillet pan, place it over medium heat, add oil and warm, add onion, and then cook for 5 minutes until golden brown.

2. Add spice mix, add remaining ingredients into the pan except for okra, stir until mixed, and then bring the mixture to a simmer.

3. Add chickpeas, stir until mixed, and then cook for 5 minutes over medium-low heat setting until thoroughly warmed.

4. Serve straight away.

Per Serving
calories: 188 | fat: 7.8g | protein: 6.5g | carbs: 26.1g | fiber: 6.5g

Walnut-Breaded Bell Peppers

Prep time: 5 minutes | Cook time: 15 minutes | Serves 2

8 ounces (227 g) walnuts, soaked overnight
¼ cup sliced green bell peppers
½ cup sliced white onions
¼ cup sliced red bell peppers
¼ cup sliced orange bell peppers
1 tablespoon onion powder

½ teaspoon sea salt
1 teaspoon dried oregano
¼ teaspoon cayenne pepper
1 teaspoon dried basil
2 tablespoons grapeseed oil
2 tablespoons spring water

1. Drain the walnuts, place them in a food processor, and then pulse until crumbled.

2. Take a skillet pan, place it over medium-high heat, add oil and when hot, add onions and all the peppers, stir in all the seasoning and then cook for 10 minutes until tender.

3. Add walnuts, stir in water and then cook for 3 to 5 minutes until hot.

4. Serve warm.

Per Serving
calories: 241 | fat: 23.8g | protein: 5.8g | carbs: 5.5g | fiber: 2.6g

Chapter 7: Salads

Spaghetti Squash "Noodles" and Broccoli Salad

Prep time: 10 minutes | Cook time: 50 minutes | Serves 4

1 spaghetti squash
2 tablespoons coconut oil
2 cups cooked broccoli florets
1 red bell pepper, seeded and cut into strips
1 scallion, chopped
1 tablespoon sesame oil
1 teaspoon red pepper flakes
2 teaspoons sea salt, divided
2 tablespoons toasted sesame seeds

1. Preheat the oven to 350°F (180°C).
2. To roast a spaghetti squash, cut the squash in half lengthwise and scrape out the seeds. Brush each half with coconut oil and season with 1 teaspoon sea salt. Place the squash halves cut-side up on a baking sheet and roast in the preheated oven for about 50 minutes, or until fork tender.
3. Prepare the spaghetti squash "noodles" by removing the inside of the roasted squash with a fork into a large bowl.
4. Add the broccoli, red bell pepper, and scallion.
5. In a small bowl, combine the sesame oil, red pepper flakes, and remaining salt. Drizzle atop the vegetables. Toss gently to combine.
6. Garnish with the sesame seeds and serve.

Per Serving
calories: 112 | fat: 5.9g | protein: 2.3g
carbs: 6.5g | fiber: 2.4g

Strawberry and Dandelion Salad

Prep time: 10 minutes | Cook time: 7 minutes | Serves 2

½ of onion, peeled, sliced
5 strawberries, sliced
2 cups dandelion greens, rinsed
1 tablespoon key lime juice
1 tablespoon grapeseed oil
¼ teaspoon salt

1. Take a medium skillet pan, place it over medium heat, add oil and let it heat until warm.
2. Add onion, season with ⅛ teaspoon salt, stir until mixed, and then cook for 3 to 5 minutes until tender and golden brown.
3. Meanwhile, take a small bowl, place slices of strawberries in it, drizzle with ½ tablespoon lime juice and then toss until coated.
4. When onions have turned golden brown, stir in remaining lime juice, stir until mixed, and then cook for 1 minute.
5. Remove pan from heat, transfer onions into a large salad bowl, add strawberries along with their juices and dandelion greens and then sprinkle with remaining salt. Toss until mixed and then serve.

Per Serving
calories: 205 | fat: 16.2g | protein: 6.9g
carbs: 10.5g | fiber: 2.7g

Caprese Salad

Prep time: 5 minutes | Cook time: 0 minutes | Serves 2

2 large heirloom tomatoes, sliced
1 avocado, sliced

1 bunch basil leaves
1 teaspoon sea salt

1. On a platter, layer 1 tomato slice, 1 avocado slice, and 1 basil leaf. Repeat the pattern with all remaining tomato slices, avocado slices, and basil leaves.
2. Season with the salt and serve.

Per Serving
calories: 126 | fat: 9.9g | protein: 1.8g
carbs: 9.2g | fiber: 4.8g

Broccoli and Tangerine Salad

Prep time: 5 minutes | Cook time: 0 minutes | Serves 4

4 cups cooked broccoli florets, cooled
2 seedless tangerines, peeled and separated
1/3 cup freshly squeezed orange

juice
2 tablespoons sesame oil
2 garlic cloves, minced
1/2 teaspoon sea salt
1/4 teaspoon red pepper flakes

1. In a large bowl, combine the broccoli and tangerine sections.
2. In a blender, combine the orange juice, sesame oil, garlic, salt, and red pepper flakes. Blend until smooth.
3. Pour the dressing over the broccoli salad. Refrigerate for 1 hour to blend the flavors.
4. Serve cold.

Per Serving (1¼ Cups)
calories: 102 | fat: 7.1g | protein: 2.7g
carbs: 13.5g | fiber: 3.4g

Root Vegetable Salad

Prep time: 15 minutes | Cook time: 0 minutes | Serves 2

1 red beet, peeled and shredded
1 golden beet, peeled and shredded
2 carrots, peeled

and shredded
2 tablespoons hazelnuts
2 tablespoons golden raisins
1/2 teaspoon sea salt

1. In a medium bowl, stir together the red beet, golden beet, carrots, hazelnuts, golden raisins, and salt.
2. Refrigerate for 15 minutes to blend the flavors. Serve.

Per Serving (1 Cup)
calories: 102 | fat: 0.2g | protein: 1.8g
carbs: 25.2g | fiber: 3.1g

Lush Summer Salad

Prep time: 5 minutes | Cook time: 0 minutes | Serves 4

4 cups chopped iceberg or romaine lettuce
2 cups cherry tomatoes, halved
1 (14.5-ounce / 411-g) can whole green beans,

drained
1/2 cup shredded carrot
1 scallion, sliced
1 cucumber, peeled and sliced
2 radishes, thinly sliced

1. In a large bowl, combine the lettuce, tomatoes, green beans, carrot, scallion, cucumber, and radishes.
2. Toss well with 2 tablespoons the dressing of choice and serve immediately.

Per Serving (2 Cups)
calories: 39 | fat: 0.3g | protein: 1.5g
carbs: 9.0g | fiber: 2.2g

Cucumber and Arugula Green Salad

Prep time: 5 minutes | Cook time: 0 minutes | Serves 2

½ cucumber, deseeded
4 ounces (113 g) arugula
⅛ teaspoon salt
1 tablespoon key

lime juice
1 tablespoon olive oil
⅛ teaspoon cayenne pepper

1. Cut the cucumber into slices, add to a salad bowl and then add arugula in it.
2. Mix together lime juice and oil until combined, pour over the salad, and then season with salt and cayenne pepper.
3. Toss until mixed and then serve.

Per Serving
calories: 143 | fat: 12.6g | protein: 1.5g
carbs: 7.9g | fiber: 1.2g

Cucumber and Mushroom Green Salad

Prep time: 5 minutes | Cook time: 0 minutes | Serves 2

½ of a medium cucumber, deseeded, chopped
6 leaves of lettuce, broke into pieces
4 mushrooms, chopped

6 cherry tomatoes, chopped
10 olives
½ of lime, juiced
1 teaspoon olive oil
¼ teaspoon salt

1. Take a medium salad bowl, place all the ingredients in it and then toss until mixed.
2. Serve straight away.

Per Serving
calories: 128 | fat: 6.8g | protein: 1.9g
carbs: 13.8g | fiber: 3.8g

Mango and Jicama Salad

Prep time: 5 minutes | Cook time: 15 minutes | Serves 1

1 mango, peeled and cut into bite-size pieces
1 cup sliced jicama
1 cup sliced bell

pepper
Juice of 1 lime
1 tablespoon chili powder

1. In a small bowl, combine mango, bell pepper, and jicama.
2. Squeeze the lime juice over the vegetables. Sprinkle with the chili powder.
3. Refrigerate for 15 minutes to allow flavors to blend and enjoy.

Per Serving
calories: 202 | fat: 1.2g | protein: 2.9g
carbs: 50.1g | fiber: 5.2g

Amaranth, Cucumber, and Chickpea Salad

Prep time: 5 minutes | Cook time: 10 minutes | Serves 2

1 small white onion, peeled, chopped
1 cup cooked amaranth
½ of cucumber, deseeded, chopped
1 cup cooked chickpeas
½ of medium

red bell pepper, chopped
⅓ teaspoon sea salt
⅛ teaspoon cayenne pepper
2 tablespoons key lime juice

1. Take a small bowl, place lime juice in it, add salt and stir until combined.
2. Place remaining ingredients in a salad bowl, drizzle with lime juice mixture, toss until mixed, and then serve.

Per Serving
calories: 215 | fat: 4.6g | protein: 6.6g
carbs: 37.1g | fiber: 8.9g

Rainbow Salad

Prep time: 10 minutes | Cook time: 0 minutes | Serves 2

1 mango, peeled, destoned, cubed	½ of green bell pepper, deseeded, sliced
¼ of onion, chopped	⅓ teaspoon salt
½ cup cherry tomatoes, halved	¼ teaspoon cayenne pepper
½ of cucumber, deseeded, sliced	¼ of key lime, juiced

1. Take a medium bowl, place the mango pieces in it, add onion, tomatoes, cucumber, and bell pepper and then drizzle with lime juice.
2. Season with salt and cayenne pepper, toss until combined, and let the salad rest in the refrigerator for a minimum of 20 minutes.
3. Serve straight away.

Per Serving
calories: 109 | fat: 0.5g | protein: 1.1g
carbs: 28.2g | fiber: 3.2g

Chickpea, Veg, and Fonio Salad

Prep time: 10 minutes | Cook time: 5 minutes | Serves 2

½ cup cooked chickpeas	½ cup fonio
¼ cup chopped cucumber	⅓ teaspoon salt
½ cup chopped red pepper	1 tablespoon grapeseed oil
½ cup cherry tomatoes, halved	⅛ teaspoon cayenne pepper
	1 key lime, juiced
	1 cup spring water

1. Take a medium saucepan, place it over high heat, pour in water, and bring it to boil.
2. Add fonio, switch heat to the low level, cook for 1 minute, and then remove the pan from heat.

3. Cover the pan with its lid, let fonio rest for 5 minutes, fluff by using a fork and then let it cool for 15 minutes.
4. Take a salad bowl, place lime juice and oil in it and then stir in salt and cayenne pepper until combined.
5. Add remaining ingredients including fonio, toss until mixed, and then serve.

Per Serving
calories: 146 | fat: 2.9g | protein: 5.9g
carbs: 24.4g | fiber: 5.4g

Wakame and Pepper Salad

Prep time: 15 minutes | Cook time: 0 minutes | Serves 2

1 cup wakame stems	lime juice
½ tablespoon chopped red bell pepper	½ tablespoon agave syrup
	½ tablespoon sesame seeds
½ teaspoon onion powder	½ tablespoon sesame oil
½ tablespoon key	

1. Place wakame stems in a bowl, cover with water, let them soak for 10 minutes, and then drain.
2. Meanwhile, prepare the dressing and for this, take a small bowl, add lime juice, onion, agave syrup and sesame oil in it and then whisk until blended.
3. Place drained wakame stems in a large dish, add bell pepper, pour in the dressing and then toss until coated.
4. Sprinkle sesame seeds over the salad and then serve.

Per Serving
calories: 105 | fat: 7.2g | protein: 3.0g
carbs: 7.9g | fiber: 1.6g

Roasted Asparagus and Mushroom Salad

Prep time: 10 minutes | Cook time: 15 minutes | Serves 2

½ bunch asparagus, trimmed
1 pint cherry tomatoes
½ cup mushrooms, halved
1 carrot, peeled and cut into bite-size pieces

1 red or yellow bell pepper, seeded and cut into bite-size pieces
1 tablespoon coconut oil
1 tablespoon garlic powder
1 teaspoon sea salt

1. Preheat the oven to 425ºF (220ºC).
2. In a bowl, add the asparagus, tomatoes, mushrooms, carrot, and bell pepper. Add the coconut oil, garlic powder, and salt. Toss to coat the vegetables evenly.
3. Transfer the vegetables to a baking pan, place in the preheated oven, and roast for 15 minutes, or until the vegetables are tender.
4. Transfer the vegetables to a large bowl. Refrigerate, if desired.
5. Divide the vegetables into two bowls and serve either warm or cold.

Per Serving (1 Cup)
calories: 133 | fat: 7.4g | protein: 3.0g
carbs: 15.2g | fiber: 4.1g

Sprouts and Kale Salad

Prep time: 5 minutes | Cook time: 0 minutes | Serves 2

2 cups kale leaves
1 cup sprouts
1 cup cherry tomato
½ of avocado, peeled, pitted, diced
1 key lime, juiced

1 teaspoon agave syrup
½ tablespoon olive oil
⅛ teaspoon cayenne pepper

1. Take a small bowl, place lime juice in it, add oil and agave syrup and then stir until mixed.
2. Take a salad bowl, place remaining ingredients in it, drizzle with the lime juice mixture and then toss until mixed.
3. Serve straight away.

Per Serving
calories: 179 | fat: 14.2g | protein: 3.6g
carbs: 13.6g | fiber: 6.2g

Basil Lettuce Salad

Prep time: 10 minutes | Cook time: 10 minutes | Serves 2

2 small heads of romaine lettuce, cut in half
1 tablespoon chopped basil
1 tablespoon chopped red onion
¼ teaspoon onion powder

½ tablespoon agave syrup
½ teaspoon salt
¼ teaspoon cayenne pepper
2 tablespoons olive oil
1 tablespoon key lime juice

1. Take a large skillet pan, place it over medium heat and when warmed, arrange lettuce heads in it, cut-side down, and then cook for 4 to 5 minutes per side until golden brown on both sides.
2. When done, transfer lettuce heads to a plate and then let them cool for 5 minutes.
3. Meanwhile, prepare the dressing and for this, place remaining ingredients in a small bowl and then stir until combined.
4. Drizzle the dressing over lettuce heads and then serve.

Per Serving
calories: 131 | fat: 2.0g | protein: 2.1g
carbs: 23.9g | fiber: 3.8g

Sea Vegetable and Seaweed Salad

Prep time: 5 minutes | Cook time: 0 minutes | Serves 2

1 cup dried sea vegetables
1 ounce (28 g) dry seaweed
1 teaspoon spirulina
1 teaspoon apple cider vinegar
1 packet stevia
1 teaspoon sesame seeds

1. Reconstitute the dried sea vegetables and seaweed according to the package directions.
2. Meanwhile, in a small bowl, mix together the spirulina, cider vinegar, and stevia.
3. Drain the sea vegetables and seaweed. Squeeze any excess moisture from them and place them in a medium bowl. Add the spirulina mixture and toss to combine.
4. Refrigerate for 1 hour to blend the flavors.
5. Top with the sesame seeds and serve.

Per Serving (1 Cup)
calories: 62 | fat: 0.2g | protein: 2.3g
carbs: 4.1g | fiber: 2.6g

Broccoli, Asparagus, and Quinoa Salad

Prep time: 5 minutes | Cook time: 0 minutes | Serves 4

1 cup cooked broccoli florets, roughly chopped
1 cup trimmed and cooked asparagus spears, roughly chopped
2 cups cooked
quinoa, cooled
½ cup water
2 tablespoons freshly squeezed lemon juice
2 tablespoons coconut oil
½ teaspoon sea salt

1. In a large bowl, combine the broccoli and asparagus.
2. Stir in the quinoa.

3. In a blender, combine the water, lemon juice, coconut oil, and salt. Blend until the ingredients emulsify. Pour the dressing over the salad. Stir to combine.
4. Refrigerate the salad for 15 minutes to chill.
5. Serve cold.

Per Serving (1 Cup)
calories: 365 | fat: 11.6g | protein: 12.2g
carbs: 53.0g | fiber: 6.1g

Pineapple Green Salad

Prep time: 10 minutes | Cook time: 0 minutes | Serves 1 to 2

For the Lime Vinaigrette:
¼ cup avocado oil
¼ cup water
2 tablespoons freshly squeezed lime juice
½ cup chopped
scallions
½ cup chopped fresh cilantro
2 garlic cloves
½ teaspoon sea salt

For Assembling:
2 to 3 cups mixed salad greens
½ cup cubed pineapple
1 cup chopped purple cabbage
Dulse flakes, for garnish (optional)

1. To Prepare the Vinaigrette
2. In a blender, blend together the avocado oil, water, lime juice, onion, cilantro, garlic, and salt until well combined. Adjust the seasonings, if necessary.
3. To Assemble the Salad
4. Plate the mixed salad greens on 1 large or 2 small plates. Top with the pineapple, purple cabbage, and dulse flakes (if using); drizzle with the dressing; and serve.

Per Serving
calories: 319 | fat: 27.6g | protein: 2.5g
carbs: 19.1g | fiber: 3.4g

Quinoa and Brussels Sprouts Salad

Prep time: 5 minutes | Cook time: 0 minutes | Serves 2

¼ cup quinoa, cooked
½ pound (227 g) Brussels sprouts, halved, diced, roasted
2 tablespoons dried cranberries
1 medium white onion, peeled, sliced caramelized
⅓ teaspoon salt
⅛ teaspoon cayenne pepper
½ orange, juiced
½ teaspoon orange zest
1 tablespoon key lime juice

1. Take a small bowl, pour orange juice and lime juice in it, add orange zest and then stir until mixed.
2. Take a salad bowl, place remaining ingredients in it, drizzle with the orange juice mixture and then toss until mixed.
3. Serve straight away.

Per Serving
calories: 191 | fat: 12.1g | protein: 4.9g
carbs: 17.8g | fiber: 2.9g

Watercress and Orange Salad

Prep time: 10 minutes | Cook time: 0 minutes | Serves 2

4 cups torn watercress
1 sliced avocado
2 thin sliced red onions
1 chopped seville orange
2 tablespoons key lime juice
2 teaspoons agave syrup
⅛ teaspoon pure sea salt
Cayenne powder, to taste
2 tablespoons olive oil

1. Prepare the avocado. cut it in half, peel, remove the seed, and slice.
2. Peel the seville orange and cut it into medium cubes.
3. Remove the skin from red onions and thinly slice.
4. Put onions, avocado, oranges and watercress in a salad bowl.
5. Combine olive oil, cayenne powder, pure sea salt, key lime juice and agave syrup together in a separate bowl, mix well.
6. Pour dressing on the top of the salad.
7. Serve immediately.

Per Serving
calories: 346 | fat: 28.4g | protein: 4.4g
carbs: 24.7g | fiber: 8.8g

Mushroom and Olive Salad

Prep time: 10 minutes | Cook time: 0 minutes | Serves 2

5 halved mushrooms
6 halved cherry (plum) tomatoes
6 rinsed lettuce leaves
10 olives
½ chopped cucumber
Juice from ½ key lime
1 teaspoon olive oil
Pure sea salt, to taste

1. Tear rinsed lettuce leaves into medium pieces and put them in a medium salad bowl.
2. Add mushroom halves, chopped cucumber, olives and cherry tomato halves into the bowl.
3. Mix well.
4. Pour olive oil and key lime juice over the salad.
5. Add pure sea salt to taste. mix it all till it is well combined.
6. Serve immediately.

Per Serving
calories: 78 | fat: 4.8g | protein: 3.1g
carbs: 8.6g | fiber: 2.4g

Spinach and Mushroom Salad

Prep time: 2 minutes | Cook time: 5 minutes | Serves 2

1 (6-ounce / 170-g) package baby spinach leaves
½ cup chopped, toasted almonds
1 tablespoon sesame oil
1 tablespoon apple cider vinegar
1 teaspoon sea salt
1 cup chopped shiitake mushrooms
Water, as needed

1. In a large bowl, combine the spinach and almonds.
2. In a small saucepan set over low heat, combine the sesame oil, cider vinegar, salt, and mushrooms. Cook for about 5 minutes, or until the mushrooms soften, adding water if needed.
3. Drizzle the mushroom dressing over the spinach. Toss well to coat the spinach leaves.
4. Serve immediately.

Per Serving (2 Cups)
calories: 272 | fat: 19.3g | protein: 10.1g
carbs: 20.1g | fiber: 7.5g

Basil Arugula Salad

Prep time: 5 minutes | Cook time: 10 minutes | Serves 2

4 ounces (113 g) arugula
½ cup cherry tomatoes, halved
¼ cup basil leaves
½ key lime, juiced
2 tablespoons
walnuts
¼ teaspoon salt
⅛ teaspoon cayenne pepper
½ tablespoon tahini butter

1. Prepare the dressing and for this, take a small bowl, place key lime juice in it, add tahini butter, salt, and cayenne pepper and then whisk until combined.

2. Take a medium bowl, place arugula, tomatoes and basil leaves in it, pour in the dressing, and then massage by using your hands.
3. Let the salad rest for 20 minutes, then taste to adjust seasoning and then serve.

Per Serving
calories: 87 | fat: 7.1g | protein: 1.5g
carbs: 6.1g | fiber: 1.2g

Fennel and Carrot Salad

Prep time: 5 minutes | Cook time: 0 minutes | Serves 4

1 cup chopped fennel
1 cup shredded carrots
¼ cup sliced almonds
3 tablespoons raisins
1 tablespoon avocado oil
1 tablespoon freshly
squeezed lemon juice
1 teaspoon apple cider vinegar
1 teaspoon Dijon or yellow mustard
1 teaspoon finely grated fresh ginger, or 1 cube frozen ginger

1. In a medium bowl, toss the fennel, carrots, almonds, and raisins to combine; set aside.
2. In a small bowl, whisk together the oil, lemon juice, vinegar, mustard, and ginger until well combined.
3. Pour the dressing over the slaw and toss until evenly coated.
4. Serve cold or at room temperature. Store any leftovers in an airtight container in the refrigerator for up to 1 week.

Per Serving (¾ cup)
calories: 166 | fat: 8.9g | protein: 4.8g
carbs: 19.1g | fiber: 6.0g

Sweet Tahini Peach Salad

Prep time: 10 minutes | Cook time: 0 minutes | Serves 1 to 2

4 tablespoons tahini
3 to 4 tablespoons brown rice syrup
¼ cup water
1 teaspoon freshly squeezed lemon juice
Pinch sea salt
1 peach, pitted and cubed
¼ cup diced red bell pepper
1 tablespoon chopped fresh cilantro
1 tablespoon diced red onion
½ jalapeño, diced
2 to 3 cups mixed salad greens

1. In a small bowl, whisk together the tahini, brown rice syrup, water, lemon juice and salt until well combined. Adjust seasonings, if necessary.
2. In another small bowl, toss together the peach, bell pepper, cilantro, onion, and jalapeño.
3. Plate the mixed salad greens on 1 large or 2 small plates. Top with the salsa, drizzle with the dressing, and enjoy.

Per Serving
calories: 302 | fat: 16.5g | protein: 6.9g carbs: 37.0g | fiber: 5.5g

Avocado and Chickpea Salad

Prep time: 10 minutes | Cook time: 20 minutes | Serves 2

½ of cucumber, deseeded, sliced
2 avocados, peeled, pitted, cubed
1 medium white onion, peeled, diced
2 cups cooked chickpeas
¼ cup chopped coriander
1 teaspoon onion powder
½ teaspoon cayenne pepper
1 teaspoon sea salt
2 tablespoons hemp seeds, shelled
1 key lime, juiced
1 tablespoon olive oil

1. Switch on the oven, then set it to 425ºF (220ºC) and let it preheat.
2. Meanwhile, take a baking sheet, place chickpeas on it, season with salt, onion powder, and pepper, drizzle with oil and then toss until combined.
3. Bake the chickpeas for 20 minutes or until golden brown and crisp and then let them cool for 10 minutes.
4. Transfer chickpeas to a bowl, add remaining ingredients and stir until combined. Serve straight away.

Per Serving
calories: 208| fat: 7.9g | protein: 6.5g carbs: 30.1g | fiber: 7.8g

Orange and Avocado Green Salad

Prep time: 5 minutes | Cook time: 0 minutes | Serves 2

1 orange, peeled, sliced
4 cups greens
½ of avocado, peeled, pitted, diced
2 tablespoons slivered red onion
½ cup cilantro
¼ teaspoon salt
¼ cup olive oil
2 tablespoons lime juice
2 tablespoons orange juice

1. Prepare the dressing and for this, place cilantro in a food processor, pour in orange juice, lime juice, and oil, add salt and then pulse until blended.
2. Tip the dressing into a mason jar. Add remaining ingredients, toss until coated, and add to a salad bowl, or serve in jar.

Per Serving
calories: 227 | fat: 18.8g | protein: 3.2g carbs: 14.5g | fiber: 6.8g

Citrus Avocado and Arugula Salad

Prep time: 5 minutes | Cook time: 0 minutes | Serves 2

4 slices of onion
½ of avocado, peeled, pitted, sliced
4 ounces (113 g) arugula
1 orange, zested, peeled, sliced
1 teaspoon agave

syrup
⅛ teaspoon salt
⅛ teaspoon cayenne pepper
2 tablespoons key lime juice
2 tablespoons olive oil

1. Distribute avocado, oranges, onion, and arugula between two plates.
2. Mix together oil, salt, cayenne pepper, agave syrup and lime juice in a small bowl and then stir until mixed.
3. Drizzle the dressing over the salad and then serve.

Per Serving
calories: 266 | fat: 24.1g | protein: 3.7g
carbs: 11.5g | fiber: 6.3g

Tofu and Watermelon Salad

Prep time: 10 minutes | Cook time: 0 minutes | Serves 4

2 tablespoons freshly squeezed lemon juice
2 tablespoons avocado oil
1 teaspoon dried oregano
½ teaspoon dried thyme
¼ teaspoon garlic powder
¼ teaspoon sea salt

8 ounces (227 g) firm tofu, cubed
¼ cup balsamic vinegar
8 dates, pitted
4 cups crisp leafy greens
1 cup cubed watermelon
¼ cup chopped fresh basil

1. In a small bowl, combine the lemon juice, oil, oregano, thyme, garlic powder, and salt. Add the tofu and let

it soak up the flavors while you make the salad.
2. In a high-speed blender, combine the vinegar and dates and blend until smooth.
3. Into each of 4 salad bowls, place 1 cup the leafy greens. Add ¼ cup the watermelon to each.
4. Using a slotted spoon, top each bowl with 2 tablespoons the vegan feta. (Store the remaining vegan feta in an airtight container in the refrigerator for up to 5 days.)
5. Garnish evenly with the basil. Drizzle a tablespoon the balsamic mixture onto each salad and serve.

Per Serving
calories: 150 | fat: 4.9g | protein: 5.9g
carbs: 21.1g | fiber: 2.9g

Avocado and Spelt Noodle Salad

Prep time: 10 minutes | Cook time: 0 minutes | Serves 2

½ cup avocado, peeled, pitted, chopped
½ cup basil leaves
½ cup cherry tomatoes
2 cups cooked spelt

noodles
1 teaspoon agave syrup
1 tablespoon key lime juice
2 tablespoons olive oil

1. Take a large bowl, place pasta in it, add tomato, avocado, and basil in it and then stir until mixed.
2. Take a small bowl, add agave syrup and salt in it, pour in lime juice and olive oil, and then whisk until combined.
3. Pour lime juice mixture over pasta, toss until combined, and then serve.

Per Serving
calories: 388 | fat: 16.5g | protein: 9.3g
carbs: 54.2g | fiber: 8.5g

Thai Green Salad

Prep time: 10 minutes | Cook time: 0 minutes | Serves 2

4 cups chopped iceberg lettuce
1 cup bean sprouts
2 carrots, cut into thin slices or spirals
1 zucchini, cut into thin strips or spirals
1 scallion, finely chopped

2 tablespoons chopped almonds
Juice of 1 lime
1 garlic clove
1 teaspoon tamarind paste
1 packet stevia
½ teaspoon sea salt

1. In a large bowl, combine the lettuce, bean sprouts, carrots, zucchini, scallion, and almonds.
2. In a small food processor bowl, add the lime juice, garlic, tamarind, stevia, and salt. Blend to combine.
3. Pour the dressing over the vegetables and mix thoroughly.
4. Divide evenly between two bowls and serve.

Per Serving (3 Cups)
calories: 80 | fat: 3.0g | protein: 2.1g
carbs: 6.5g | fiber: 5.4g

Spinach Strawberry Salad with Lemon Vinaigrette

Prep time: 5 minutes | Cook time: 0 minutes | Serves 4

For the Lemon Vinaigrette:
3 tablespoons avocado oil
Juice of 1 small lemon
1 teaspoon Dijon or yellow mustard

¼ teaspoon ground turmeric
⅛ teaspoon sea salt
1 teaspoon maple syrup (optional)

For the Salad:
4 cups baby spinach
1 cup halved strawberries

¼ cup sliced almonds

1. To Make the Lemon Vinaigrette
2. In a small bowl, whisk together the oil, lemon juice, mustard, turmeric, and salt until well combined. Add the maple syrup (if using) and mix well.
3. To Make the Salad
4. In a large bowl, toss the baby spinach, strawberries, and almonds.
5. Drizzle the dressing over the salad and gently toss to combine. Serve immediately. Or, if you are planning to serve later, store the undressed salad and the dressing in separate airtight containers in the refrigerator and add the dressing to the salad when ready to serve.

Per Serving
calories: 161 | fat: 13.8g | protein: 2.9g
carbs: 6.1g | fiber: 3.2g

Avocado and Quinoa Salad

Prep time: 10 minutes | Cook time: 0 minutes | Serves 2

1 cup cooked quinoa, cooled
1 avocado, cut into cubes
1 cup cherry tomatoes, halved
1 cup cucumber, peeled and diced
¼ cup chopped

cilantro
1 tablespoon garlic powder
1 tablespoon onion powder
1 teaspoon sea salt
1 tablespoon freshly squeezed lemon juice

1. In a large bowl, stir together the quinoa, avocado, tomatoes, cucumber, cilantro, garlic powder, onion powder, salt, and lemon juice.
2. Chill for 15 minutes to allow the flavors to blend.
3. Serve immediately, or keep refrigerated for 2 to 3 days.

Per Serving (2 Cups)
calories: 435 | fat: 14.7g | protein: 13.5g
carbs: 63.5g | fiber: 9.8g

Asparagus Salad with Cashew Dressing

Prep time: 10 minutes | Cook time: 5 minutes | Serves 1 to 2

For the Salad:

1 teaspoon avocado oil
24 asparagus stalks, diced
½ cup diced onion
3 garlic cloves, crushed
½ teaspoon sea salt
¼ teaspoon freshly ground black pepper

For the Dressing:

½ cup raw cashews
½ cup water
2 tablespoons freshly squeezed lemon juice
¼ teaspoon sea salt
⅛ teaspoon freshly ground black pepper

For Assembling:

2 cups mixed salad greens

1. To Prepare the Asparagus Mixture
2. In a large skillet over medium heat, heat the avocado oil. Add the asparagus, onion, garlic, salt, and pepper, and sauté for 5 to 7 minutes, or until the onion is soft.
3. To Prepare the Dressing
4. In a high-speed blender, blend together half the asparagus mixture with the cashews, water, lemon juice, salt, and pepper until creamy and smooth.
5. To Assemble the Salad
6. Plate the mixed salad greens on 1 large or 2 small plates. Top with the remaining asparagus mixture, drizzle with the dressing, and enjoy.

Per Serving

calories: 409 | fat: 27.7g | protein: 16.8g
carbs: 32.4g | fiber: 8.3g

Rainbow Salad with Citrus Mango Salsa

Prep time: 5 minutes | Cook time: 0 minutes | Serves 4

For the Citrus Mango Salsa:

2 cups chopped mango
1 cup chopped fennel
⅓ cup chopped scallions
¼ cup fresh chopped basil
3 tablespoons freshly squeezed lemon juice
¼ teaspoon sea salt

For the Rainbow Salad:

1 (15-ounce / 425-g) can low-sodium chickpeas, drained (liquid reserved) and rinsed
½ cup chopped bell pepper
1 teaspoon chopped fresh cilantro, for garnish

1. To Make the Citrus Mango Salsa
2. In a medium bowl, combine the mango, fennel, scallions, basil, lemon juice, and salt and toss well. For best results, cover and refrigerate for several hours or up to overnight to let the flavors meld.
3. To Make the Rainbow Salad
4. In a large bowl, combine the chickpeas, bell pepper, and ¼ cup the salsa. (Store the remaining salsa in an airtight container in the refrigerator for 5 to 7 days.)
5. Garnish the salad with the cilantro and serve.

Per Serving

calories: 125 | fat: 2.1g | protein: 5.9g
carbs: 23.9g | fiber: 5.8g

Kale and Roasted Beet Salad

Prep time: 10 minutes | Cook time: 20 minutes | Serves 1 to 2

4 small beets, peeled and cut into small cubes
1 teaspoon avocado oil
¼ teaspoon dried rosemary
⅛ teaspoon garlic powder
Pinch sea salt
Pinch freshly ground black pepper
2 cups bite-size stemmed curly kale
pieces
⅛ teaspoon sea salt
2 tablespoons avocado oil
1 tablespoon freshly squeezed lemon juice
1 tablespoon brown rice syrup
1 garlic clove, crushed
Pinch sea salt
Pinch freshly ground black pepper

1. Preheat the oven to 400ºF (205ºC). Line a baking pan with parchment paper.
2. In a small bowl, toss the beets with the avocado oil to coat. Sprinkle with the rosemary, garlic powder, salt, and pepper, and toss to coat. Transfer the beets to the prepared baking pan and roast for 15 to 20 minutes, or until slightly crispy.
3. Meanwhile, in a medium bowl, sprinkle the kale with the salt, and gently massage the kale with your hands, scrunching it until it becomes soft and slightly limp, about 3 minutes. Transfer to a serving dish.
4. In a small bowl, whisk together the avocado oil, lemon juice, brown rice syrup, garlic, salt, and pepper until well combined.
5. Add the beets to the bowl with the kale, and drizzle with the dressing. Transfer to 1 large or 2 small plates and enjoy.

Per Serving
calories: 253 | fat: 16.7g | protein: 3.5g
carbs: 25.0g | fiber: 5.3g

Sweet Potato Salad with Jalapeño Dressing

Prep time: 10 minutes | Cook time: 25 minutes | Serves 1 to 2

For the Sweet Potatoes:
3 medium sweet potatoes, peeled and cubed
2 tablespoons avocado oil
2 garlic cloves, crushed
1 teaspoon ground paprika
½ teaspoon sea salt

For the Jalapeño Dressing:
1 cup water
1 cup raw cashews
¼ cup fresh cilantro leaves
½ to 1 jalapeño
2 tablespoons freshly squeezed lime juice
½ teaspoon sea salt

For Assembling:
2 cups mixed salad greens

1. Preheat the oven to 350ºF (180ºC). Line a baking sheet with parchment paper.
2. To Prepare the Sweet Potatoes
3. In a medium bowl, toss together the sweet potatoes, avocado oil, garlic, paprika, and salt.
4. Spread the sweet potato cubes evenly on the prepared baking pan, and bake for 25 minutes, or until soft.
5. To Prepare the Jalapeño Dressing
6. Meanwhile, in a high-speed blender, blend together the water, cashews, cilantro, jalapeño, lime juice, and salt until smooth.
7. To Assemble
8. Plate the mixed salad greens on 1 large or 2 small plates. Top with the warm sweet potatoes, drizzle with the dressing, and enjoy.

Per Serving
calories: 709 | fat: 46.4g | protein: 14.6g
carbs: 67.1g | fiber: 9.6g

Red Lentil Pasta and Veggie Salad

Prep time: 15 minutes | Cook time: 15 minutes | Serves 2 to 4

2 cups red lentil pasta
¼ cup avocado oil
2 tablespoons apple cider vinegar
1 tablespoon freshly squeezed lemon juice
1 teaspoon dried oregano
2 pinches sea salt
2 pinches freshly ground black pepper

1 tablespoon avocado oil
6 asparagus stalks, diced
1 cup diced orange bell pepper
$^1/_3$ cup diced red onion
½ zucchini, sliced
½ summer squash, sliced
2 garlic cloves, crushed

1. Cook the pasta according to package directions.
2. While the pasta cooks, in a small bowl, whisk together the avocado oil, vinegar, lemon juice, oregano, salt, and pepper until well combined. Adjust the seasonings, if necessary.
3. In a skillet over medium-high heat, heat the avocado oil. Add the asparagus, bell pepper, onion, zucchini, squash, and garlic, and sauté for 2 to 3 minutes, or just until soft.
4. In a large bowl, toss the cooked pasta, veggies, and dressing until well combined. Transfer to 2 large or 4 small plates and enjoy.

Per Serving
calories: 262 | fat: 17.8g | protein: 3.0g | carbs: 24.0g | fiber: 4.8g

Watercress and Cucumber Salad

Prep time: 5 minutes | Cook time: 0 minutes | Serves 2

2 cups torn watercress
½ sliced cucumber
1 tablespoon key lime juice

2 tablespoons olive oil
Pure sea salt, to taste
Cayenne powder, to taste

1. Pour key lime juice and olive oil into a salad bowl. mix them well to combine.
2. Slice the cucumber and add to the bowl.
3. Tear watercress and add to the bowl.
4. Sprinkle cayenne powder and pure sea salt on top according to your liking.
5. Mix thoroughly.
6. Serve immediately.

Per Serving
calories: 125 | fat: 13.5g | protein: 0.8g carbs: 1.1g | fiber: 0.2g

Chapter 8: Snacks

Tarragon Almond Crackers

Prep time: 10 minutes | Cook time: 15 minutes | Makes 60 small crackers

3 tablespoons water
1 tablespoon ground flaxseed
2 cups almond flour
1 tablespoon fresh chopped tarragon
1 tablespoon avocado oil
½ teaspoon sea salt
½ teaspoon freshly ground black pepper
¼ teaspoon garlic powder

1. Preheat the oven to 350ºF (180ºC). Line a baking sheet with parchment paper.
2. To prepare a flax egg, in a large bowl, whisk together the water and flaxseed.
3. Add the almond flour, tarragon, avocado oil, salt, pepper, and garlic powder, and stir until well combined.
4. Transfer the mixture to the prepared baking sheet. Using your hands, form the dough into a ball, then place another piece of parchment paper on the top of the ball.
5. Using a rolling pin over the parchment paper, roll out the dough to about ¼-inch thickness.
6. Use a knife or pizza cutter to cut the dough into 60 (1½-inch-by-1½-inch) squares.
7. Bake for 12 to 14 minutes, or until the crackers are slightly golden on top. Flip them over and bake for another minute or 2.
8. Cool and serve.

Per Serving (10 Crackers)
calories: 184 | fat: 3.1g | protein: 0.6g
carbs: 38.5g | fiber: 2.0g

Avocado Fries

Prep time: 10 minutes | Cook time: 15 minutes | Makes 16 fries

½ cup almond flour
2 tablespoons nutritional yeast
¼ to ½ teaspoon garlic powder
¼ to ½ teaspoon ground paprika,
plus more for sprinkling
¼ to ½ teaspoon sea salt
2 avocados, slightly underripe
½ cup almond milk

1. Preheat the oven to 420ºF (216ºC). Line a baking sheet with parchment paper.
2. In a small bowl, stir together the almond flour, nutritional yeast, garlic powder, paprika, and salt until well combined.
3. Halve and pit the avocados, and quarter each half from pole to pole. Peel off the skin.
4. Add the almond milk to another small bowl.
5. Dip an avocado slice into first the milk and then the coating mixture, gently tossing it to make sure it is completely covered, and place on the prepared baking sheet. Repeat with the remaining avocado slices.
6. Bake for 15 to 17 minutes, taking care not to overcook or burn them.
7. Remove from the oven, sprinkle with additional paprika, and serve immediately.

Per Serving (2 Fries)
calories: 127 | fat: 7.8g | protein: 2.4g
carbs: 14.1g | fiber: 4.5g

Tahini Parsley and Zucchini Hummus

Prep time: 10 minutes | Cook time: 0 minutes | Makes 1 cup

¼ cup water
2 tablespoons avocado oil
2 teaspoons freshly squeezed lemon juice
3 tablespoons tahini
1 cup chopped fresh parsley sprigs, plus more (optional) for garnish
½ zucchini, peeled
3 garlic cloves, crushed
½ teaspoon sea salt

1. In a high-speed blender, blend to combine the water, avocado oil, lemon juice, tahini, parsley, zucchini, garlic, and salt until creamy.
2. Garnish with the extra parsley (if using), and serve.

Per Serving (¼ Cup)
calories: 138 | fat: 13.2g | protein: 2.6g carbs: 4.3g | fiber: 1.6g

Broccoli Bites

Prep time: 5 minutes | Cook time: 20 minutes | Makes 3 cups

½ cup almond flour
½ cup nutritional yeast
½ teaspoon garlic powder
½ teaspoon sea salt
¼ to ½ teaspoon ground cayenne pepper (optional)
3 cups bite-size broccoli florets
2 tablespoons avocado oil

1. Preheat the oven to 400ºF (205ºC). Line a baking sheet with parchment paper.
2. In a small bowl, stir together the almond flour, nutritional yeast, garlic powder, salt, and cayenne pepper (if using).
3. In a medium bowl, toss the broccoli with the avocado oil to coat.

4. Sprinkle half the seasoning mixture over the broccoli, gently toss until all pieces are coated, and bake for 10 minutes.
5. Remove from the oven, and transfer the broccoli pieces back to the medium bowl. Sprinkle with the remaining half of the seasoning mix, and toss to coat.
6. Return to the oven for an additional 5 to 10 minutes, and serve.

Per Serving (1 Cup)
calories: 274 | fat: 12.0g | protein: 14.4g carbs: 33.6g | fiber: 10.5g

Kale Chips

Prep time: 5 minutes | Cook time: 10 minutes | Serves 1 to 2

4 or 5 stalks curly kale, stemmed and torn (2 cups, packed)
1 tablespoon avocado oil
1 tablespoon nutritional yeast
¼ teaspoon sea salt

1. Preheat the oven to 350ºF (180ºC). Line a baking sheet with parchment paper.
2. In a medium bowl, toss the kale with the avocado oil to coat.
3. Sprinkle the nutritional yeast and salt over the kale, and toss to coat.
4. Transfer the kale to the prepared baking sheet, and bake for 5 to 6 minutes. Turn them over and bake for an additional 5 to 6 minutes, or until they are crispy, taking care not to burn them.
5. Cool and serve.

Per Serving
calories: 89 | fat: 7.6g | protein: 3.1g carbs: 3.9g | fiber: 2.2g

Cashew Stuffed Mushrooms

Prep time: 5 minutes | Cook time: 5 minutes | Makes 12 mushrooms

12 cremini mushrooms, stemmed	1 cup raw cashews
1½ teaspoons avocado oil	2 garlic cloves
Pinch sea salt	¼ cup freshly squeezed lemon juice
Pinch freshly ground black pepper	1 teaspoon apple cider vinegar
	¼ teaspoon sea salt

1. Rinse and dry the mushroom caps.
2. In a medium skillet over medium heat, heat the avocado oil. Add the mushroom caps, sprinkle with salt and pepper, and sauté for 2 to 4 minutes, or until they soften. Discard any liquid that may accumulate.
3. In a high-speed blender, blend to combine the cashews, garlic, lemon juice, vinegar, and salt until a thick paste forms.
4. Spoon the mixture evenly among the 12 mushroom caps and serve.

Per Serving (2 Mushrooms)
calories: 462 | fat: 35.6g | protein: 14.2g carbs: 29.8g | fiber: 3.6g

Hearty Party Snack Mix

Prep time: 5 minutes | Cook time: 10 minutes | Serves 6

Cooking spray	2 tablespoons garlic powder
1 cup raw almonds	2 tablespoons onion powder
½ cup flaked unsweetened coconut	1 teaspoon chili powder
1 cup raisins	1 teaspoon ground ginger
1 cup dried pineapple pieces	1 teaspoon sea salt
½ cup roasted peas	1 tablespoon coconut oil
½ cup pumpkin seeds	

1. Preheat the oven to 425°F (220°C).
2. Spray a large baking pan with cooking spray.
3. In a medium bowl, combine the almonds, coconut, raisins, pineapple, peas, pumpkin seeds, garlic powder, onion powder, chili powder, ginger, salt, and coconut oil.
4. Spread the mix in an even layer in the baking pan.
5. Bake for 10 minutes in the preheated oven, being careful that it doesn't burn.
6. Remove from the oven and cool before serving.

Per Serving (¾ Cup)
calories: 228 | fat: 12.6g | protein: 5.2g carbs: 27.8g | fiber: 4.0g

Paprika Almonds

Prep time: 5 minutes | Cook time: 5 minutes | Makes 1 cup

1 teaspoon avocado oil	½ teaspoon garlic powder
1 cup raw almonds	½ to ¾ teaspoon sea salt
1 teaspoon ground paprika	

1. In a large skillet over medium heat, heat the avocado oil. Add the almonds, and toss gently until all the almonds are covered with the oil.
2. Add the paprika, garlic powder, and salt, tossing gently after each addition to make sure it is evenly distributed and all the almonds are covered. Adjust seasonings as desired. Continue cooking and gently tossing for about 5 minutes.
3. Remove from the heat and allow to cool before serving.

Per Serving (¼ Cup)
calories: 220 | fat: 19.1g | protein: 7.7g carbs: 8.3g | fiber: 4.7g

Baked Walnut Apple

Prep time: 10 minutes | Cook time: 55 minutes | Serves 2

4 apples, large, cored, sliced	3 tablespoons agave syrup
⅛ teaspoon ground cloves	1 tablespoon chopped walnuts

1. Switch on the oven, then set it to 350ºF (180ºC) and let it preheat.
2. Meanwhile, take a large bowl, place apple slices in it, drizzle with agave syrup and then toss until evenly coated.
3. Take a small bowl, place nuts in it, add cloves, and then stir until mixed.
4. Sprinkle nuts mixture over the apple and let it rest for 5 minutes or more until apples start releasing their juices.
5. Take a medium casserole dish, arrange apple slices on it, and then bake for 15 minutes.
6. Cover the casserole dish with foil and then continue baking for 40 minutes until bubbly.
7. Let apples cool for 10 minutes and then serve.

Per Serving
calories: 345 | fat: 6.5g | protein: 1.6g
carbs: 77.9g | fiber: 6.1g

Burro Banana Fries

Prep time: 5 minutes | Cook time: 10 minutes | Serves 2

4 baby burro bananas, peeled, cut in squares	½ of medium green bell pepper, cored, chopped
¼ teaspoon salt	2 teaspoons grapeseed oil
½ of a medium onion, peeled, chopped	¼ teaspoon cayenne pepper

1. Take a medium skillet pan, place it over medium-low heat, add oil and when hot, add burro banana pieces and then cook for 3 minutes or until beginning to brown.
2. Then turn the burro banana pieces, add remaining ingredients, stir until mixed, and then continue cooking for 5 to 7 minutes until onions have caramelized.
3. Serve straight away.

Per Serving
calories: 131 | fat: 6.6g | protein: 1.1g
carbs: 19.8g | fiber: 2.9g

Zucchini Walnut Pancakes

Prep time: 10 minutes | Cook time: 8 minutes | Serves 2

1 cup spelt flour	homemade
½ cup grated zucchini	1 tablespoon date sugar
¼ cup chopped walnuts	1 tablespoon grapeseed oil
1 cup walnut milk,	

1. Take a medium bowl, place flour in it, add date sugar, and then stir until mixed.
2. Add mashed burro banana and milk in it, whisk until smooth batter comes together, and then fold in nuts and zucchini until just mixed.
3. Take a large skillet pan, place it over medium-high heat, add oil and when hot, pour the batter in it in portion and then shape each portion into a pancake.
4. Cook each pancake for 3 to 4 minutes per side and then serve.

Per Serving
calories: 131 | fat: 4.1g | protein: 3.2g
carbs: 20.9g | fiber: 2.8g

Coconut Banana Coins

Prep time: 2 minutes | Cook time: 5 minutes | Serves 1

2 tablespoons shredded unsweetened coconut
Pinch sea salt

2 tablespoons coconut oil
1 banana, peeled and sliced into ¼-inch-thick slices

1. On a plate, combine the coconut and salt.
2. In a medium pan set over medium heat, melt the coconut oil.
3. Press each banana slice into the coconut mixture until coated.
4. Gently place each slice into the heated coconut oil. Sauté for 2 minutes, flip, and continue cooking for 2 to 3 minutes on the second side.
5. Cool slightly and serve warm.

Per Serving
calories: 172 | fat: 6.2g | protein: 1.4g
carbs: 28.5g | fiber: 4.5g

Buffalo Cauliflowers

Prep time: 10 minutes | Cook time: 25 minutes | Serves 4

1 teaspoon sea salt
1 teaspoon garlic powder
1 teaspoon onion powder
1 cauliflower head,

broken into florets
2 tablespoons coconut oil, melted
½ teaspoon cayenne pepper

1. Preheat the oven to 450ºF (235ºC).
2. In a small bowl, mix together the salt, garlic powder, and onion powder.
3. Season the cauliflower with the spice mix. Place the seasoned cauliflower in a baking pan and into the preheated oven. Bake for 10 minutes, turn the cauliflower over, and bake for 10 minutes more.

4. In a large bowl, while the cauliflower is baking, combine the coconut oil and cayenne pepper.
5. Transfer the hot cauliflower to the large bowl with the coconut oil. Toss to coat thoroughly and return the cauliflower to the baking pan.
6. Bake for 5 minutes more, until the sauce is absorbed.
7. Remove from the oven and let sit for 10 minutes before serving.

Per Serving (1 Cup)
calories: 81 | fat: 6.8g | protein: 1.4g
carbs: 4.5g | fiber: 1.6g

Okra Pod Bites

Prep time: 5 minutes | Cook time: 20 minutes | Serves 2

12 okra pods, cut into ¼-inch-thick slices
1 teaspoon avocado oil

½ teaspoon sea salt
¼ teaspoon freshly ground black pepper

1. Preheat the oven to 450ºF (235ºC). Line a baking sheet with parchment paper.
2. In a medium bowl, toss the okra and avocado oil to coat. Season with salt and pepper, and toss again.
3. Place the seasoned okra on the prepared baking sheet in a single layer, and roast for 15 to 20 minutes, flipping halfway through and taking care not to overbake.
4. These are best served hot from the oven.

Per Serving
calories: 44 | fat: 2.4g | protein: 1.4g
carbs: 5.5g | fiber: 2.4g

Oregano Almond Breadsticks with Garlic Topping

Prep time: 5 minutes | Cook time: 20 minutes | Makes 12 pieces

3 tablespoons water
1 tablespoon ground flaxseed
2 cups almond flour
1 tablespoon avocado oil
1 tablespoon chopped fresh oregano
½ teaspoon sea salt
½ teaspoon freshly ground black pepper

For the Topping:
4 garlic cloves, crushed
1 tablespoon chopped fresh oregano
⅛ teaspoon sea salt
⅛ teaspoon freshly ground black pepper
1 tablespoon avocado oil

1. Preheat the oven to 350ºF (180ºC). Line a baking sheet with parchment paper.
2. To prepare a flax egg, in a small bowl, whisk together the water and flaxseed until well blended.
3. In a medium bowl, stir together the flax egg, almond flour, avocado oil, oregano, salt, and pepper until well combined.
4. Transfer the mixture to the prepared baking sheet, and gather the mixture together to form a ball. Take another sheet of parchment paper, lay it on top of the ball, and using a rolling pin over the paper, roll the dough into a 5-by-8-inch rectangle shape.
5. In a small bowl, stir together the garlic, oregano, salt, pepper, and avocado oil until well combined. Pour the topping mixture over the dough, and use the back of a spoon to spread it evenly.
6. Bake for 18 to 20 minutes, or until the edges are golden brown.
7. Remove from the oven, slice into 12 pieces, and serve.

Per Serving (2 Pieces)
calories: 335 | fat: 29.3g | protein: 10.7g
carbs: 12.9g | fiber: 7.3g

Chinese Spicy Green Beans

Prep time: 5 minutes | Cook time: 15 minutes | Serves 4

1 pound (454 g) green beans, ends trimmed
1 teaspoon coconut oil
1 teaspoon sesame oil
½ teaspoon red pepper flakes
2 garlic cloves, finely chopped
1 teaspoon chopped fresh ginger
½ teaspoon sea salt

1. Adjust the oven racks so that the top rack is closest to the broiler.
2. Preheat the broiler.
3. Place the green beans in a baking pan in a single layer. Broil the beans for about 10 minutes, or until they start to show black flecks. Remove the beans from the broiler and transfer them to a large bowl. Set aside.
4. In a small saucepan, add the coconut oil, sesame oil, red pepper flakes, garlic, ginger, and salt. Warm the mixture over medium heat until it begins to shimmer and turn red. Turn off the heat.
5. Pour the warm sauce over the green beans and toss well to combine.
6. Return the beans to the baking pan and place back under the broiler for 5 minutes.
7. Remove from the oven, place the green beans on a serving platter, and serve warm.

Per Serving (4 Ounces Sauced Green Beans)
calories: 62 | fat: 2.4g | protein: 2.1g
carbs: 8.9g | fiber: 3.8g

Jicama Fries

Prep time: 10 minutes | Cook time: 40 minutes | Serves 2

½ jicama, peeled and cut into 32 (¼-inch-thick) sticks
1 tablespoon avocado oil
¼ to ½ teaspoon chipotle powder
¼ teaspoon garlic powder
¼ to ½ teaspoon sea salt
¼ teaspoon freshly ground black pepper

1½ cups raw cashews
½ cup coconut milk (boxed)
¾ cup roughly chopped scallions
¼ cup vegetable broth
1 tablespoon apple cider vinegar
1 tablespoon freshly squeezed lemon juice
1 garlic clove
½ teaspoon sea salt

1. Preheat the oven to 400°F (205°C). Line a baking sheet with parchment paper.
2. In a medium bowl, toss the jicama sticks with the avocado oil to coat.
3. Add the chipotle powder, garlic powder, salt, and pepper, and toss again to coat. Adjust the seasonings, if necessary.
4. Transfer the jicama sticks to the prepared baking sheet and spread in a single layer.
5. Bake for 20 minutes, flip them over, and bake for an additional 15 to 20 minutes.
6. Meanwhile in a high-speed blender, blend together the cashews coconut milk, scallions, broth, vinegar, lemon juice, garlic, and salt until creamy and smooth. Adjust the seasonings, if necessary, and serve.

Per Serving
calories: 779 | fat: 57.7g | protein: 19.2g
carbs: 49.5g | fiber: 11.3g

Avocado and Tomato Spelt Toast

Prep time: 5 minutes | Cook time: 0 minutes | Serves 2

2 slices of spelt bread, toasted
1 avocado, peeled, pitted, mashed
½ cup cherry

tomato halves
½ teaspoon salt
2 teaspoons key lime juice

1. Place avocado in a bowl, add lime juice, and then mash until smooth.
2. Spread mashed avocado evenly on top of each toast and then scatter cherry tomatoes.
3. Sprinkle salt over tomatoes and then serve.

Per Serving
calories: 190 | fat: 10.9g | protein: 2.9g
carbs: 19.9g | fiber: 5.5g

Almond Stuffed Dates

Prep time: 2 minutes | Cook time: 0 minutes | Serves 1

4 small dates, pitted
4 teaspoons unsweetened finely

shredded coconut
4 whole raw almonds

1. With a small paring knife, slice each date open lengthwise.
2. Press 1 teaspoon the coconut into the center of each date.
3. Place an almond into the center of the coconut.
4. Sprinkle any remaining coconut over the dates and enjoy.

Per Serving
calories: 160 | fat: 6.9g | protein: 2.1g
carbs: 24.9g | fiber: 3.8g

Avocado and Cucumber Sushi Roll

Prep time: 10 minutes | Cook time: 0 minutes | Serves 1

2 nori seaweed squares
¼ cup cooked brown rice, divided
Wasabi, for garnish (optional)
½ avocado, diced, divided

½ cucumber, peeled and diced, divided
1 teaspoon sesame oil, divided
1 teaspoon toasted sesame seeds, divided

1. Place one nori sheet in your hand. Add 2 tablespoons brown rice, wasabi (if using), half of the diced avocado, and half of the diced cucumber.
2. Drizzle with ½ teaspoon sesame oil. Sprinkle ½ teaspoon the sesame seeds.
3. Wrap the nori around the filling so it looks like a cone. Carefully set on a plate.
4. Repeat with the remaining ingredients for a second hand roll.
5. Serve and eat immediately.

Per Serving
calories: 458 | fat: 27.2g | protein: 7.1g | carbs: 51.2g | fiber: 9.6g

Tomato Mini Mushroom Pizzas

Prep time: 5 minutes | Cook time: 15 minutes | Serves 4

Cooking spray
1 (6-ounce / 170-g) can organic tomato paste
1 tablespoon garlic powder
1 tablespoon onion powder
1 teaspoon dried oregano

4 tablespoons sun-dried tomatoes
½ teaspoon sea salt, plus a pinch, divided
4 portobello mushroom caps, gills removed
4 slices fresh tomato

1. Preheat the oven to 350ºF (180ºC).
2. Spray a baking pan with cooking spray.
3. In a small bowl, mix together the tomato paste, garlic powder, onion powder, oregano, sun-dried tomatoes, and sea salt.
4. Evenly divide the tomato mixture into the 4 mushroom caps. Top each with 1 tomato slice and a pinch of the sea salt.
5. Transfer the pizzas to the baking pan, place the pan in the preheated oven, and bake for 15 minutes, or until the pizzas are hot and bubbly.

Per Serving (Mini Pizza)
calories: 68 | fat: 1.2g | protein: 2.8g | carbs: 13.5g | fiber: 2.6g

Cauliflower Popcorn

Prep time: 10 minutes | Cook time: 30 minutes | Serves 4

1 cauliflower head, separated into small florets

3 tablespoons coconut oil
1 teaspoon sea salt

1. Preheat the oven to 400ºF (205ºC).
2. In a large bowl, combine the cauliflower, coconut oil, and salt.
3. Transfer the cauliflower to a baking sheet and spread it evenly into a single layer.
4. Place the sheet in the preheated oven and roast for about 30 minutes, until golden brown and slightly crisp.

Per Serving (1 Cup)
calories: 106 | fat: 10.2g | protein: 1.2g | carbs: 3.4g | fiber: 1.6g

Roasted Red Pepper Eggplant Rollups

Prep time: 15 minutes | Cook time: 13 minutes | Serves 6

1 (12-ounce / 340-g) jar packed-in-water roasted red peppers
¼ onion, chopped
1 garlic clove
1 tablespoon freshly squeezed lemon juice
¼ teaspoon red pepper flakes

3 fresh basil leaves
2 eggplants, tops removed, thinly sliced lengthwise (about 24 slices)
Cooking spray
2 teaspoons sea salt

1. In a food processor, add the roasted red peppers, onion, garlic, lemon juice, red pepper flakes, and basil. Pulse until blended but still chunky.
2. Preheat the grill to medium, or preheat the broiler.
3. Lay the eggplant slices on a baking sheet and spray with cooking spray. Sprinkle with the salt.
4. Transfer the eggplant slices to the grill and grill for 3 minutes, or until grill marks form. If you don't have a grill, place the baking sheet in the broiler and broil instead.
5. Remove the eggplant from the grill and transfer it back to the baking sheet (or remove the baking sheet from the oven).
6. If using a grill, preheat the oven to 375ºF (190ºC).
7. If using a broiler for the eggplant slices, reduce the oven heat to 375ºF (190ºC).
8. Place 1 to 2 tablespoons tapenade on one end of each eggplant slice. Roll the slices up and over the filling, finishing seam-side down. Put the sheet back in the oven and bake the rolls for 10 minutes or until heated.
9. Serve warm.

Per Serving (4 Rolls)
calories: 36 | fat: 0.2g | protein: 1.3g | carbs: 8.6g | fiber: 3.4g

Rosemary Mushroom Pâté

Prep time: 5 minutes | Cook time: 15 minutes | Serves 6

Cooking spray
1 onion, chopped
2 pounds (907 g) fresh mushrooms, any kind, finely chopped
2 garlic cloves, minced

1 tablespoon chopped fresh parsley
¼ teaspoon finely chopped fresh rosemary
½ teaspoon sea salt
1 tablespoon freshly squeezed lemon juice

1. Spray a medium saucepan with the cooking spray. Add the onion and cook over medium heat for about 5 minutes, or until translucent.
2. Add the mushrooms and garlic to the pan. Cook for 10 minutes more, until cooked through.
3. Remove from the heat and transfer the mixture to a food processor. Add the parsley, rosemary, salt, and lemon juice. Pulse to a desired consistency.
4. Serve as suggested above.

Per Serving (¼ Cup)
calories: 42 | fat: 0.5g | protein: 4.9g | carbs: 7.0g | fiber: 3.4g

Golden Chickpea Nuggets

Prep time: 10 minutes | Cook time: 30 minutes | Serves 2

2 cups cooked chickpeas
½ teaspoon salt

1 teaspoon onion powder
$^1/_3$ cup and 1 tablespoon bread crumbs

1. Switch on the oven, then set it to 350ºF (180ºC) and let it preheat.
2. Meanwhile, place chickpeas in a food processor and then pulse until crumbled.
3. Tip the chickpeas in a bowl, add remaining ingredients in it except for $^1/_3$ cup breadcrumbs and then stir until a chunky mixture comes together.
4. Shape the mixture into evenly sized balls, shape each ball into the nugget, arrange on a baking sheet greased with oil and then bake for 15 minutes per side until golden brown.
5. Serve straight away.

Per Serving
calories: 292 | fat: 4.0g | protein: 20.0g | carbs: 26.9g | fiber: 3.5g

Chapter 9: Soups and Stews

Carrot and Fennel Soup

Prep time: 10 minutes | Cook time: 30 minutes | Serves 2 to 4

6 carrots
1 cup chopped onion
1 fennel bulb, cubed
2 garlic cloves, crushed
2 tablespoons

avocado oil
1 teaspoon sea salt
1 teaspoon freshly ground black pepper
2 cups almond milk, plus more if desired

1. Preheat the oven to 400ºF (205ºC). Line a baking sheet with parchment paper.
2. Cut the carrots into thirds, and then cut each third in half. Transfer to a medium bowl.
3. Add the onion, fennel, garlic, and avocado oil, and toss to coat. Season with the salt and pepper, and toss again.
4. Transfer the vegetables to the prepared baking sheet, and roast for 30 minutes.
5. Remove from the oven and allow the vegetables to cool.
6. In a high-speed blender, blend together the almond milk and roasted vegetables until creamy and smooth. Adjust the seasonings, if necessary, and add additional milk if you prefer a thinner consistency.
7. Pour into 2 large or 4 small bowls and enjoy.

Per Serving
calories: 415 | fat: 22.8g | protein: 11.8g
carbs: 45.0g | fiber: 10.2g

Herbed Lentil and Potato Coconut Stew

Prep time: 10 minutes | Cook time: 30 minutes | Serves 4

2 tablespoons avocado oil
½ cup diced onion
2 garlic cloves, crushed
1 to 1½ teaspoons sea salt
1 teaspoon freshly ground black pepper
1 cup dry lentils
2 carrots, sliced

1 cup peeled and cubed potato
1 celery stalk, diced
2 fresh oregano sprigs, chopped
2 fresh tarragon sprigs, chopped
5 cups vegetable broth, divided
1 (13.5-ounce / 383-g) can full-fat coconut milk

1. In a large soup pot over medium-high heat, heat the avocado oil. Add the onion, garlic, salt, and pepper, and sauté for 3 to 5 minutes, or until the onion is soft.
2. Add the lentils, carrots, potato, celery, oregano, tarragon, and 2½ cups vegetable broth, and stir.
3. Bring to a boil, reduce the heat to medium-low, and cook, stirring frequently and adding additional vegetable broth a half cup at a time to make sure there is enough liquid for the lentils and potatoes to cook, for 20 to 25 minutes, or until the potatoes and lentils are soft.
4. Remove from the heat, and stir in the coconut milk. Pour into 4 soup bowls and enjoy.

Per Serving
calories: 619 | fat: 34.4g | protein: 20.8g
carbs: 64.2g | fiber: 12.5g

Avocado and Cucumber Gazpacho

Prep time: 5 minutes | Cook time: 0 minutes | Serves 2

1 avocado, peeled, pitted, cold	½ of key lime, juiced
1 cucumber, deseeded, unpeeled, cold	2 cups spring water, chilled
½ cup basil leaves, cold	1½ teaspoon sea salt

1. Place all the ingredients into the jar of a high-speed food processor or blender and then pulse until smooth.
2. Tip the soup into a medium bowl and then chill for a minimum of 1 hour.
3. Divide the soup evenly between two bowls, top with some more basil and then serve.

Per Serving
calories: 191 | fat: 15.1g | protein: 3.9g carbs: 15.2g | fiber: 5.9g

Kale, Soursop and Zucchini Soup

Prep time: 5 minutes | Cook time: 45 minutes | Serves 2

1 cup chopped kale	onions
2 soursop leaves, rinsed, rip in half	1 cup diced green bell peppers
½ cup summer squash cubes	2 teaspoons sea salt
1 cup chayote squash cubes	½ tablespoon basil
½ cup zucchini cubes	¼ teaspoon cayenne pepper
½ cup wild rice	½ tablespoon oregano
½ cup diced white	6 cups spring water

1. Take a medium pot, place it over medium-high heat, add soursop leaves, pour in 1½ cup water, and then boil for 15 minutes, covering the pan with lid.

2. When done, remove eaves from the broth, switch heat to medium level, add remaining ingredients into the pot, stir until mixed, and then cook for 30 minutes or more until done.
3. Serve straight away.

Per Serving
calories: 225 | fat: 4.9g | protein: 5.7g carbs: 37.9g | fiber: 3.5g

Vegetable and Spelt Noodle Soup

Prep time: 5 minutes | Cook time: 12 minutes | Serves 2

½ onion, peeled, cubed	¼ cup basil leaves
½ green bell pepper, chopped	1 pack spelt noodles, cooked
½ zucchini, grated	¼ teaspoon salt
4 ounces (113 g) sliced mushrooms, chopped	⅛ teaspoon cayenne pepper
½ cup cherry tomatoes	½ key lime, juiced
	1 tablespoon grapeseed oil
	2 cups spring water

1. Take a medium saucepan, place it over medium heat, add oil and when hot, add onion and then cook for 3 minutes or more until tender.
2. Add cherry tomatoes, bell pepper, and mushrooms, stir until mixed, and then continue cooking for 3 minutes until soft.
3. Add grated zucchini, season with salt, cayenne pepper, pour in the water, and then bring the mixture to a boil.
4. Then switch heat to the low level, add cooked noodles and then simmer the soup for 5 minutes.
5. When done, ladle soup into two bowls, top with basil leaves, drizzle with lime juice and then serve.

Per Serving
calories: 266 | fat: 1.9g | protein: 3.8g carbs: 56.9g | fiber: 13.5g

Coconut Mushroom Soup

Prep time: 5 minutes | Cook time: 20 minutes | Serves 2

2 cups baby Bella mushrooms, diced
½ cup diced red onions
1 cup vegetable broth
1½ cups soft-jelly
coconut milk
½ teaspoon sea salt
¼ teaspoon cayenne pepper
2 teaspoons grapeseed oil

1. Take a medium saucepan, place it over medium-high heat, add oil and when hot, add onion, mushrooms, season with salt and pepper, and then cook for 3 to 4 minutes until vegetables turn tender.
2. Then add soy sauce, pour in milk and broth, stir until mixed and bring it to a boil.
3. Switch heat to medium-low level and then simmer the soup for 15 minutes until thickened to the desired level.
4. Serve straight away.

Per Serving
calories: 101 | fat: 1.9g | protein: 2.1g
carbs: 17.9g | fiber: 1.9g

Tarragon Kamut Vegetable Soup

Prep time: 5 minutes | Cook time: 32 minutes | Serves 2

6 tablespoons kamut berries
1 cup chopped white onion
½ cup chopped squash
½ cup cooked chickpeas
1 cup vegetable broth, homemade
¼ teaspoon
cayenne pepper
½ tablespoon chopped tarragon
1 bay leaf
1 teaspoon chopped thyme
1 tablespoon olive oil
1 cup spring water, boiling

1. Place kamut in a small bowl, pour in the boiling water, and let it stand for 30 minutes.
2. Then take a medium pot, place it over medium heat, add oil and when hot, add onion, stir in thyme and tarragon and then cook for 5 minutes until tender.
3. Drain kamut, add to the pot, add bay leaves, pour in the vegetable broth, and then bring it to boil.
4. Cover the pot with its lid, simmer for 20 to 30 minutes, then stir in cayenne pepper and cook for 5 minutes.
5. Remove bay leaf, add chickpeas, and then cook for 2 minutes.
6. Serve straight away.

Per Serving
calories: 349 | fat: 8.8g | protein: 11.3g
carbs: 57.2g | fiber: 7.7g

Zucchini Green Soup

Prep time: 10 minutes | Cook time: 10 minutes | Serves 2

2 cups leafy greens
1 small zucchini, sliced
1 small white onion, peeled, sliced
1 medium green bell pepper, cored, sliced
2 ½ cups spring water
¾ teaspoon salt
¼ teaspoon cayenne pepper
1 teaspoon dried basil

1. Take a medium pot, place it over medium heat, add all the ingredients, stir until mixed, and then cook for 5 to 10 minutes until the vegetables turn tender-crisp.
2. Remove pot from heat, purée the soup by using an immersion blender and then serve.

Per Serving
calories: 130 | fat: 0.3g | protein: 1.2g
carbs: 27.9g | fiber: 4.6g

Basil Squash Soup

Prep time: 5 minutes | Cook time: 25minutes | Serves 2

½ of medium white onion, peeled, cubed
2 cups cubed squash
¼ cup basil leaves
½ cup soft-jelly coconut cream
⅛ teaspoon sea salt
⅛ teaspoon cayenne pepper
1 tablespoon grapeseed oil
1 cup vegetable broth, homemade

1. Take a medium saucepan, place it over medium heat, add oil and when hot, add onion, and then cook for 5 minutes or until softened.
2. Add squash, cook for 10 minutes until golden and begin to soften, pour in the vegetable broth, season with salt and pepper and then bring the soup to boil.
3. Switch heat to medium level and then simmer the soup for 10 minutes until squash turns very soft.
4. Remove pan from heat, purée it by using a stick blender until smooth, and then garnish with basil.
5. Serve straight away.

Per Serving
calories: 184 | fat: 14.5g | protein: 2.0g carbs: 13.5g | fiber: 2.8g

Kale and Chickpea Curry

Prep time: 5 minutes | Cook time: 10 minutes | Serves 2

2 cups cooked chickpeas
⅔ teaspoon salt
1 cup kale leaves
⅔ cup soft-jelly
coconut cream
2 tablespoons grapeseed oil
⅓ teaspoon cayenne pepper

1. Switch on the oven, then set it to 425ºF (220ºC) and let it preheat.

2. Then take a medium baking sheet, spread chickpeas on it, drizzle with 1 tablespoon oil, sprinkle with all the seasonings and then bake for 15 minutes until roasted.
3. Then take a frying pan, place it over medium heat, add remaining oil and when hot, add kale and cook for 5 minutes.
4. Add roasted chickpeas, pour in the cream, stir until mixed and then simmer for 4 minutes, squashing chickpeas slightly.
5. Serve straight away.

Per Serving
calories: 521 | fat: 37.9g | protein: 14.8g carbs: 25.9g | fiber: 8.2g

Onion and Squash Soup

Prep time: 5 minutes | Cook time: 35 minutes | Serves 2

2 large white onions, peeled, sliced
½ cup cubed squash
1 sprig of thyme
1 tablespoon grapeseed oil
2 cups spring water
½ teaspoon salt
¼ teaspoon cayenne pepper

1. Take a medium pot, place it over medium heat, add oil and when hot, add onion and cook for 10 minutes.
2. Add thyme sprig, switch heat to the low level and then cook onions for 15 to 20 minutes until soft, covering the pan with its lid.
3. Add remaining ingredients, stir until mixed and simmer for 5 minutes.
4. Ladle soup into bowls and then serve.

Per Serving
calories: 75 | fat: 2.2g | protein: 2.4g carbs: 13.2g | fiber: 2.6g

Tarragon Cashew Coconut Soup

Prep time: 10 minutes | Cook time: 10 minutes | Serves 1 to 2

1 tablespoon avocado oil
½ cup diced onion
3 garlic cloves, crushed
¼ plus ⅛ teaspoon sea salt
¼ plus ⅛ teaspoon freshly ground black pepper
1 (13.5-ounce /

383-g) can full-fat coconut milk
1 tablespoon freshly squeezed lemon juice
½ cup raw cashews
1 celery stalk
2 tablespoons chopped fresh tarragon

1. In a medium skillet over medium-high heat, heat the avocado oil. Add the onion, garlic, salt, and pepper, and sauté for 3 to 5 minutes, or until the onion is soft.
2. In a high-speed blender, blend together the coconut milk, lemon juice, cashews, celery, and tarragon with the onion mixture until smooth. Adjust seasonings, if necessary.
3. Pour into 1 large or 2 small bowls and enjoy immediately, or transfer to a medium saucepan and warm on low heat for 3 to 5 minutes before serving.

Per Serving
calories: 752 | fat: 71.4g | protein: 11.0g
carbs: 28.5g | fiber: 6.4g

Cucumber and Zucchini Soup

Prep time: 5 minutes | Cook time: 0 minutes | Serves 1 to 2

1 cucumber, peeled
½ zucchini, peeled
1 tablespoon freshly squeezed lime juice
1 tablespoon fresh

cilantro leaves
1 garlic clove, crushed
¼ teaspoon sea salt

1. In a blender, blend together the cucumber, zucchini, lime juice, cilantro, garlic, and salt until well combined. Add more salt, if necessary.
2. Pour into 1 large or 2 small bowls and enjoy immediately, or refrigerate for 15 to 20 minutes to chill before serving.

Per Serving
calories: 49 | fat: 0.7g | protein: 2.7g
carbs: 9.7g | fiber: 2.5g

Chickpea Green Soup

Prep time: 5 minutes | Cook time: 25 minutes | Serves 2

½ cup cooked, chickpeas
½ of a medium white onion, peeled, diced
½ of a large zucchini, chopped
1 cup kale leaves
1 cup squash cubes
¾ teaspoon salt

¾ tablespoon chopped thyme, fresh
¾ tablespoon tarragon, fresh
2 cups vegetable broth, homemade
1½ cup spring water

1. Take a saucepan, place it over medium-high heat, pour in the ¼ cup broth, add zucchini, onion, and thyme and then cook for 4 minutes.
2. Pour in remaining broth and water, bring it to a boil, switch heat to the low level, and then simmer for 10 to 15 minutes until tender.
3. Add remaining ingredients, stir until mixed, and then continue cooking for 10 minutes or more until cooked.
4. Serve straight away.

Per Serving
calories: 185 | fat: 0.4g | protein: 6.9g
carbs: 30.8g | fiber: 5.9g

Jalapeño-Lime Coconut Soup

Prep time: 5 minutes | Cook time: 5 minutes | Serves 2

2 tablespoons avocado oil
½ cup diced onions
3 garlic cloves, crushed
¼ teaspoon sea salt
1 (13.5-ounce / 383-g) can full-fat coconut milk
1 tablespoon freshly squeezed lime juice
½ to 1 jalapeño
2 tablespoons fresh cilantro leaves

1. In a medium skillet over medium-high heat, heat the avocado oil. Add the onion, garlic, and salt, and sauté for 3 to 5 minutes, or until the onions are soft.
2. In a blender, blend together the coconut milk, lime juice, jalapeño, and cilantro with the onion mixture until creamy.
3. Pour into 1 large or 2 small bowls and enjoy.

Per Serving
calories: 611 | fat: 62.4g | protein: 5.3g
carbs: 16.3g | fiber: 5.2g

Watermelon and Jalapeño Gazpacho

Prep time: 5 minutes | Cook time: 0 minutes | Serves 1 to 2

2 cups cubed watermelon
¼ cup diced onion
¼ cup packed cilantro leaves
½ to 1 jalapeño
2 tablespoons freshly squeezed lime juice

1. In a blender or food processor, pulse to combine the watermelon, onion, cilantro, jalapeño, and lime juice only long enough to break down the ingredients, leaving them very finely diced and taking care to not overprocess.

2. Pour into 1 large or 2 small bowls and enjoy.

Per Serving
calories: 57 | fat: 0.3g | protein: 1.2g
carbs: 14.4g | fiber: 1.1g

Zucchini, Spinach, and Quinoa Soup

Prep time: 5 minutes | Cook time: 25 minutes | Serves 4

2 tablespoons avocado oil
¼ teaspoon dried oregano
¼ teaspoon dried thyme
⅛ teaspoon sea salt
1 large onion, chopped
2 large zucchini, peeled and chopped
1 cup low-sodium vegetable broth
1 cup water
1 cup baby spinach
6 large fresh basil leaves
⅓ cup cooked quinoa (optional)
Juice of 1 lemon

1. In a soup pot, heat the oil on medium heat for 1 minute, then add the oregano, thyme, and salt and cook for 30 seconds.
2. Add the onion, cover, and cook for 7 to 8 minutes, stirring regularly, until softened.
3. Add the zucchini. Cook for another 12 minutes, or until the zucchini is soft.
4. Add the broth and water and cook for another 3 minutes, until warmed.
5. Toss in the spinach and basil and cook until just wilted.
6. Transfer the mixture to a food processor and process until puréed.
7. Add the quinoa (if using). Season with the lemon juice and serve.

Per Serving
calories: 141 | fat: 11.2g | protein: 3.1g
carbs: 10.1g | fiber: 3.1g

Berry Mint Soup

Prep time: 5 minutes | Cook time: 0 minutes | Serves 1 to 2

¼ cup unrefined whole cane sugar, such as Sucanat
¼ cup water, plus more if desired
1 cup mixed berries (raspberries, blackberries, blueberries)
½ cup water
1 teaspoon freshly squeezed lemon juice
8 fresh mint leaves

1. In a small saucepan over medium-low, heat the sugar and water, stirring continuously for 1 to 2 minutes, until the sugar is dissolved. Cool.
2. In a blender, blend together the cooled sugar water with the berries, water, lemon juice, and mint leaves until well combined.
3. Transfer the mixture to the refrigerator and allow to chill completely, about 20 minutes.
4. Ladle into 1 large or 2 small bowls and enjoy.

Per Serving
calories: 109 | fat: 0.4g | protein: 0.8g
carbs: 28.3g | fiber: 4.0g

Basil Zucchini and Avocado Soup

Prep time: 5 minutes | Cook time: 0 minutes | Serves 2

2 large zucchini, chopped
1 medium avocado
1 medium bell pepper
½ cup low-sodium vegetable broth
½ cup water
¼ cup chopped fennel
6 fresh basil leaves, plus 2 small leaves
for garnish
2 teaspoons chopped fresh rosemary
1 garlic clove, peeled, or 1 cube frozen garlic
⅛ teaspoon sea salt
1½ teaspoons hulled pumpkin seeds, toasted, for garnish

1. In a high-speed blender or food processor, combine the zucchini, avocado, bell pepper, broth, water, fennel, basil, rosemary, garlic, and salt and blend until puréed.
2. Pour the soup into bowls. Garnish each with a small basil leaf and the pumpkin seeds, and serve.

Per Serving
calories: 225 | fat: 14.1g | protein: 8.2g
carbs: 23.9g | fiber: 10.1g

Potato and Broccoli Soup

Prep time: 10 minutes | Cook time: 25 minutes | Serves 2 to 4

1 tablespoon avocado oil
½ cup diced onion
2 garlic cloves, crushed
3 cups vegetable broth
1 (13.5-ounce / 383-g) can full-fat
coconut milk
2 cups peeled and cubed potatoes
3 cups bite-size broccoli florets
1 teaspoon sea salt
1½ teaspoons freshly ground black pepper

1. In a large skillet over medium-high heat, heat the avocado oil. Add the onion and garlic, and sauté for 2 to 3 minutes, or until the onions are soft.
2. Add the vegetable broth, coconut milk, potatoes, broccoli, salt, and pepper, and continue to cook for 18 to 20 minutes, or until the potatoes are soft. Remove from the heat and cool.
3. In a blender, blend the cooled soup until smooth.
4. Adjust the seasonings, if necessary. Pour into 2 large or 4 small bowls and enjoy.

Per Serving
calories: 339 | fat: 27.9g | protein: 5.2g
carbs: 22.1g | fiber: 5.2g

Butternut Squash Coconut Soup

Prep time: 5 minutes | Cook time: 15 minutes | Serves 2

2 medium butternut squash, peeled, deseeded, chopped
1 medium white onion, peeled, chopped

2 cups soft-jelly coconut milk
$2/3$ teaspoon sea salt
1 cup spring water

1. Take a large saucepan, place it over medium-high heat, pour in water, and then bring it to a boil.
2. Stir in salt, and add vegetables and then cook for 5 to 10 minutes until vegetables turn tender.
3. Remove pan from heat, add milk and then purée by using an immersion blender until smooth.
4. Serve straight away.

Per Serving
calories: 133 | fat: 4.7g | protein: 2.2g
carbs: 23.5g | fiber: 1.2g

Mushroom and Tomato Coconut Soup

Prep time: 5 minutes | Cook time: 10 minutes | Serves 2

1½ cup sliced mushrooms
8 cherry tomatoes, chopped
1 medium onion, peeled, sliced
¾ cup vegetable broth, homemade
6 teaspoons spice mix

¼ teaspoon salt
½ tablespoon grapeseed oil
¼ teaspoon cayenne pepper
¾ cup tomato sauce, alkaline
6 tablespoons soft-jelly coconut milk

1. Take a large skillet pan, place it over medium heat, add oil and warm, add onion, and then cook for 5 minutes until golden brown.

2. Add spice mix, add remaining ingredients into the pan except for okra, stir until mixed, and then bring the mixture to a simmer.
3. Add mushrooms, stir until mixed, and then cook for 10 to 15 minutes over medium-low heat setting until cooked.
4. Serve straight away.

Per Serving
calories: 190 | fat: 3.3g | protein: 2.2g
carbs: 36.6g | fiber: 3.6g

Wild Rice, Mushroom, and Leek Soup

Prep time: 10 minutes | Cook time: 55 minutes | Serves 1 to 2

$1/3$ cup wild rice
1 cup sliced cremini mushrooms
½ cup sliced leeks, white part only
3 cups water
2 tablespoons

organic white miso
¼ to ½ teaspoon freshly ground black pepper
Sliced scallions, for garnish

1. Prepare the wild rice according to the package directions.
2. In a medium soup pot over high heat, bring the sliced mushrooms, leeks, and water to a boil. Boil for 8 to 10 minutes, or until the mushrooms are soft.
3. Add the cooked wild rice, miso, and black pepper. Using the back side of a spoon, mash the miso on the side of the pot to break it down, and then stir it in.
4. Remove from the heat. Ladle into 1 large or 2 small bowls, garnish with the chopped scallions, and enjoy.

Per Serving
calories: 144 | fat: 1.5g | protein: 7.1g
carbs: 27.5g | fiber: 3.4g

Creamy Mushroom Clam Chowder

Prep time: 15 minutes | Cook time: 30 minutes | Serves 4

For the Mushroom Clams:
½ cup roughly chopped shiitake mushrooms
1 teaspoon coconut

oil
¼ cup water
½ teaspoon celery seed

For the Soup Base:
½ medium onion, chopped
3 medium carrots, peeled and chopped
2 celery stalks, finely chopped

1 teaspoon dried thyme
3 cups vegetable broth
1 sheet nori, finely crumbled

For the Cream Base:
1 cup lightly steamed cauliflower
¾ cup unsweetened almond milk
¼ teaspoon sea salt

To make the Mushroom Clams
1. In a large pot set over medium high heat, add the mushrooms and the coconut oil. Sauté for 3 minutes. Add the water and celery seed, stirring until the water is absorbed.
2. Remove from the heat and transfer the mushrooms to a plate.

To Make the Soup Base
1. In the same pot over medium heat, sauté the onion, carrots, celery, and thyme for about 5 minutes, or until the onion is softened. Add some of the broth, if needed.
2. Then, add any remaining broth and the nori and bring to a boil.
3. To Make the Cream Base
4. In a blender or food processor, add the cauliflower, almond milk, and salt. Blend to combine. If the mixture is too thick, add some of the soup base to thin. Blend until smooth.

To Assemble the Chowder
1. Add the mushroom mix and the cream base to the soup base. Stir well to combine.

2. Heat for 5 minutes, or until warm, and serve.

Per Serving (1 Cup)
calories: 98 | fat: 3.3g | protein: 6.6g
carbs: 10.9g | fiber: 2.5g

Cauliflower and Roasted Garlic Soup

Prep time: 10 minutes | Cook time: 35 minutes | Serves 1 to 2

4 cups bite-size cauliflower florets
5 garlic cloves
1½ tablespoons avocado oil
¾ teaspoon sea salt
½ teaspoon freshly

ground black pepper
1 cup almond milk
1 cup vegetable broth, plus more if desired

1. Preheat the oven to 450ºF (235ºC). Line a baking sheet with parchment paper.
2. In a medium bowl, toss the cauliflower and garlic with the avocado oil to coat. Season with the salt and pepper, and toss again.
3. Transfer to the prepared baking sheet, and roast for 30 minutes. Cool before adding to the blender.
4. In a high-speed blender, blend together the cooled vegetables, almond milk, and vegetable broth until creamy and smooth. Adjust the salt and pepper, if necessary, and add additional vegetable broth if you prefer a thinner consistency.
5. Transfer to a medium saucepan, and lightly warm on medium-low heat for 3 to 5 minutes.
6. Ladle into 1 large or 2 small bowls and enjoy.

Per Serving
calories: 278 | fat: 16.2g | protein: 10.6g
carbs: 26.7g | fiber: 6.0g

Herbed Carrot and Potato Stew

Prep time: 10 minutes | Cook time: 50 minutes | Serves 4

1 tablespoon avocado oil
1 cup onion, diced
2 garlic cloves, crushed
1 teaspoon sea salt
1 teaspoon freshly ground black pepper
3 cups vegetable broth, plus more if desired

2 cups water, plus more if desired
3 cups sliced carrot
1 large potato, cubed
2 celery stalks, diced
1 teaspoon dried oregano
1 dried bay leaf

1. In a medium soup pot over medium heat, heat the avocado oil. Add the onion, garlic, salt, and pepper, and sauté for 2 to 3 minutes, or until the onion is soft.
2. Add the vegetable broth, water, carrot, potato, celery, oregano, and bay leaf, and stir. Bring to a boil, reduce the heat to medium-low, and cook for 30 to 45 minutes, or until the potatoes and carrots are soft.
3. Adjust the seasonings, if necessary, and add additional water or vegetable broth, if a soupier consistency is preferred, in half-cup increments.
4. Ladle into 4 soup bowls and enjoy.

Per Serving
calories: 188 | fat: 5.2g | protein: 5.7g | carbs: 31.5g | fiber: 5.2g

Kale and Yellow Onion Soup

Prep time: 10 minutes | Cook time: 20 minutes | Serves 2 to 4

1 tablespoon avocado oil
2 cups thinly sliced yellow onions (3 medium)
1 teaspoon unrefined whole cane sugar, such as Sucanat
1 cup vegetable broth
2 cups water

2 tablespoons coconut aminos
2 garlic cloves, crushed
½ teaspoon dried thyme
½ teaspoon sea salt
3 kale stalks, stemmed and cut into ribbons (about 2 cups)

1. In a medium soup pot over medium-high heat, heat the avocado oil. Add the onions and sauté for 3 to 5 minutes, or until the onions begin to get soft.
2. Add the sugar and continue to sauté, stirring continuously, for 8 to 10 minutes, or until the onions are slightly caramelized.
3. Add the vegetable broth, water, coconut aminos, garlic, thyme, and salt. Reduce the heat to medium-low, and simmer for 5 to 7 minutes. Adjust seasonings, if necessary.
4. Add the kale and leave over the heat just long enough for the kale to wilt.
5. Remove from the heat, ladle into 2 large or 4 small bowls, and serve.

Per Serving
calories: 136 | fat: 9.1g | protein: 3.7g | carbs: 11.7g | fiber: 2.7g

Pear and Ginger Soup

Prep time: 10 minutes | Cook time: 15 minutes | Serves 1 to 2

2 teaspoons avocado oil
½ cup diced onions
2 garlic cloves, crushed
1 cup vegetable broth
2 cups water
¼ cup coconut milk (boxed)

2 peeled and cubed pears
1-inch piece fresh ginger root, minced
¼ teaspoon sea salt
Sliced radishes, for garnish (optional)
Chopped scallions, for garnish (optional)

1. In a large skillet over medium-high heat, heat the avocado oil. Add the onion and garlic, and sauté for 2 to 3 minutes, or until the onions are soft.
2. Add the vegetable broth, water, coconut milk, pears, ginger, and salt, and cook on medium-high heat for 8 to 10 minutes, or until the pears are soft. Remove from the heat and cool.
3. Transfer the soup to a blender, and blend until well combined. Adjust seasonings, if necessary.
4. Pour immediately into 1 large or 2 small bowls, garnish with the radishes and scallions (if using), and enjoy, or return the soup to the stove top to lightly warm on low heat before serving.

Per Serving
calories: 224 | fat: 13.0g | protein: 4.1g | carbs: 26.4g | fiber: 7.2g

Chayote Mushroom and Hemp Milk Stew

Prep time: 10 minutes | Cook time: 40 minutes | Serves 2

$2/_3$ cup chayote squash cubes
1 cups sliced mushrooms
$1/_3$ cup diced white onions
½ cup chickpea flour
$1/_3$ cup vegetable broth, homemade
$1/_3$ tablespoon onion powder

$2/_3$ teaspoon sea salt
$2/_3$ teaspoon dried basil
$1/_3$ teaspoon crushed red pepper
2 cups spring water
½ tablespoon grapeseed oil
$1/_3$ cup hemp milk, homemade

1. Take a medium pot, place it over medium-high heat, add oil and when hot, add onion and mushroom, and then cook for 5 minutes.
2. Switch heat to medium level, pour in 1 cup water, milk, and broth, add chayote and all the seasoning, stir until mixed, and then bring it to a simmer, covering the pan with lid.
3. Pour remaining water into a food processor, add chickpea flour, pulse until blended, add to the pot and then stir until mixed.
4. Switch heat to the low level, simmer for 30 minutes, and then serve.

Per Serving
calories: 174 | fat: 8.9g | protein: 2.1g | carbs: 19.9g | fiber: 2.1g

Carrot and Celery Soup

Prep time: 15 minutes | Cook time: 1 hour 10 minutes | Serves 4

Cooking spray
1 large onion, roughly chopped
2 large carrots, peeled and roughly chopped
2 large celery stalks (with leaves), roughly chopped

1 parsnip, peeled and roughly chopped
5 garlic cloves, smashed
1 leek, cleaned well and roughly chopped
9 cups water
2 bay leaves
2 teaspoons sea salt

1. Spray the bottom of a large stockpot with cooking spray. Place the pot over medium-low heat, add the onion, and sauté for about 5 minutes, stirring constantly.
2. Add the carrots, celery, parsnip, garlic, and leek to the pot. Sauté for another 3 minutes.
3. Add the water, bay leaves, and salt. Simmer for 1 hour.
4. Remove from the heat and cool slightly. Strain out the vegetables, leaving only the broth.
5. To serve, add back some of the vegetables if you wish and warm the soup to the desired temperature.

Per Serving (2 Cups)
calories: 71 | fat: 0.1g | protein: 1.7g | carbs: 11.4g | fiber: 2.1g

Lush Pepper Soup

Prep time: 5 minutes | Cook time: 10 minutes | Serves 2 to 4

1 teaspoon avocado oil
¼ cup diced onions
2 garlic cloves, crushed
2 cups diced red bell peppers
2 cups vegetable broth

½ to 1 jalapeño, seeded and diced
1 teaspoon sea salt
½ cup small-diced red bell peppers
½ cup small-diced yellow bell peppers

1. To a skillet over medium-high heat, add the avocado oil, onions, garlic, and red bell peppers, and sauté for 2 to 3 minutes, or until the onions are soft; allow to cool.
2. In a blender, blend together the sautéed mixture, vegetable broth, jalapeño, and salt until everything is well combined and completely liquid; adjust seasonings to your preference.
3. Transfer the soup to a medium bowl, and stir in the diced red and yellow bell peppers.
4. Cover and refrigerate for 20 to 30 minutes to cool or chill overnight.
5. Ladle into 2 large or 4 small bowls and enjoy.

Per Serving
calories: 83 | fat: 2.4g | protein: 3.1g | carbs: 13.4g | fiber: 3.0g

Asparagus and Artichoke Soup

Prep time: 5 minutes | Cook time: 20 minutes | Makes 4 cups

½ cup diced onion
1 tablespoon avocado oil
2 garlic cloves, crushed
1 cup cubed potatoes
8 stalks asparagus, cut into bite-size pieces

2 cups vegetable broth
½ to ¾ teaspoon sea salt
½ teaspoon ground black pepper
2 cups almond milk
1 can artichoke hearts, stemmed and halved

1. In a medium skillet, sauté the onion, avocado oil, and garlic over medium-high heat for 2 to 3 minutes, or until the onion is soft.
2. Transfer the sautéed mixture to a medium-size saucepan and add the potatoes, asparagus, vegetable broth, salt, and pepper; simmer over medium-high heat for 18 to 20 minutes, or until the potatoes are soft. Add extra vegetable broth, if needed, to keep the liquid level between ½ to 1 inch over the contents in the saucepan. Remove from the heat and allow to cool.
3. In a blender, blend the cooled soup mixture, almond milk, and artichokes until everything is well combined and the soup is smooth. Adjust seasonings to your preference and add extra almond milk or vegetable broth to thin it out, if you prefer.
4. Return the soup to the saucepan and lightly warm on low heat before serving.

Per Serving (1 Cup)
calories: 242 | fat: 8.8g | protein: 11.2g | carbs: 33.7g | fiber: 8.8g

Bok Choy, Broccolini, and Brown Rice Soup

Prep time: 5 minutes | Cook time: 10 minutes | Serves 2

3 cups vegetable broth
1 cup chopped bok choy

1 bunch broccolini, chopped roughly
½ cup cooked brown rice

1. In a medium saucepan set over medium heat, place the broth, bok choy, broccolini, and brown rice. Bring to a simmer and cook for 10 minutes, or until the vegetables are cooked until tender. Serve.

Per Serving
calories: 229 | fat: 4.1g | protein: 11.3g | carbs: 41.0g | fiber: 9.7g

Apple and Sweet Pumpkin Soup

Prep time: 5 minutes | Cook time: 25 minutes | Serves 2

1 medium apple, cored and sliced
½ cup chopped fennel
1½ cups water, divided
1 cup canned unsweetened pumpkin purée
¾ cup low-sodium vegetable broth
4 small dates, pitted
2 teaspoons grated fresh ginger, or 2 cubes frozen ginger

¼ teaspoon ground cinnamon
¼ teaspoon curry powder
⅛ teaspoon dried thyme
⅛ teaspoon sea salt
⅛ teaspoon ground cumin
4 teaspoons raisins, for garnish
2 teaspoons fennel seeds, toasted, for garnish

1. In a saucepan, combine the apples, fennel, and ½ cup water. Cover and cook on low for about 25 minutes, until the apples and fennel are softened.
2. In a food processor, combine the apple-fennel mixture, pumpkin, remaining 1 cup water, the broth, dates, ginger, cinnamon, curry powder, thyme, salt, and cumin. Process until puréed.
3. Pour the soup into two bowls and garnish each with 2 teaspoons the raisins and 1 teaspoon the toasted fennel seeds.
4. Serve immediately or let cool and serve at room temperature.

Per Serving
calories: 222 | fat: 4.9g | protein: 5.9g | carbs: 45.8g | fiber: 10.9g

Lemony Tomato and Carrot Soup

Prep time: 5 minutes | Cook time: 35 minutes | Serves 2

1 (15-ounce / 425-g) can no-sodium-added diced tomatoes, drained
¾ cup chopped carrots
1 tablespoon avocado oil
¼ teaspoon sea salt

1 cup water
½ cup low-sodium vegetable broth
2 tablespoons chopped fresh cilantro
1 tablespoon freshly squeezed lemon juice

1. Preheat the oven to 400°F (205°C).
2. In a glass baking dish, combine the tomatoes, carrots, oil, and salt and mix well.
3. Bake the tomato-carrot mixture for 35 minutes, or until caramelized, then carefully transfer to a food processor.
4. Add the water and broth, and purée until smooth.
5. Garnish with the cilantro and add the lemon juice to taste.

Per Serving
calories: 132 | fat: 7.1g | protein: 2.1g | carbs: 14.9g | fiber: 4.2g

Chapter 10: Desserts

Peach and Banana Muffin

Prep time: 10 minutes | Cook time: 15 minutes | Serves 2

²/₃ cup spelt flour homemade
½ of peach, chopped
1 teaspoon mashed burro banana
²/₃ tablespoons chopped walnuts
6½ tablespoons walnut milk,
¹/₁₆ teaspoon salt
2²/₃ tablespoon date sugar
²/₃ tablespoon spring water, warmed
²/₃ teaspoon key lime juice

1. Switch on the oven, then set it to 400ºF (205ºC) and let it preheat.
2. Meanwhile, peel the peach, cut it in half, remove the pit and then cut one half of peach in ½-inch pieces, reserving the other half of peach for later use.
3. Take a medium bowl, pour in the milk, and then whisk in mashed burro banana and lime juice until well combined.
4. Take a separate medium bowl, place flour in it, add salt and date sugar, stir until mixed, whisk in milk mixture until smooth, and then fold in peached until mixed.
5. Take 4 silicone muffin cups, grease them with oil, fill them evenly with the prepared batter and then sprinkle walnuts on top.
6. Bake the muffins for 10 to 15 minutes until the top is nicely golden brown and inserted toothpick into each muffin comes out clean.
7. When done, let muffins cool for 10 minutes and then serve.

Per Serving
calories: 76 | fat: 3.2g | protein: 1.0g
carbs: 14.2g | fiber: 0.8g

Banana and Blueberry Sea Moss Pudding

Prep time: 5 minutes | Cook time: 0 minutes | Serves 2

2 burro bananas, peeled
2 cups blueberries
6 tablespoons sea moss gel
½ cup spring water

1. Plug in a high-speed food processor or blender and add all the ingredients in its jar except for water.
2. Cover the blender jar with its lid, pulse until smooth, and then slowly blend in water until thickened to the desire level.
3. Serve straight away.

Per Serving
calories: 98 | fat: 0.6g | protein: 0.8g
carbs: 23.2g | fiber: 2.7g

Sapote and Nut Pudding

Prep time: 15 minutes | Cook time: 0 minutes | Serves 4

1 to 2 cups black sapote
¼ cup agave syrup
½ cup soaked brazil nuts (overnight or
for at least 3 hours)
1 tablespoon hemp seeds
½ cup spring water

1. Cut 1 to 2 cups black sapote in half.
2. Remove all seeds. You should have 1 full cup de-seeded fruit.
3. Put all ingredients into a blender and blend until smooth.
4. Serve and enjoy.

Per Serving
calories: 274 | fat: 12.8g | protein: 4.1g
carbs: 41.0g | fiber: 6.2g

Nutty Blueberry and Date Energy Balls

Prep time: 10 minutes | Cook time: 0 minutes | Serves 2

¼ cup blueberries
¼ cup dried dates
1 cup soft-jelly coconut, shredded
¼ cup walnuts
½ teaspoon date sugar
½ tablespoon agave syrup
$1/_{16}$ teaspoon salt

1. Place walnuts in a food processor and then pulse until the mixture resembles a fine powder.
2. Then add berries, coconut, date sugar and dates, pulse until just mixed and then slowly blend in agave syrup until the soft paste comes together.
3. Spoon the mixture into a medium bowl, chill it for a minimum of 30 minutes and then roll the mixture into balls, 1 tablespoon mixture per ball.
4. Roll the balls into some more coconut and then serve.

Per Serving
calories: 120 | fat: 8.1g | protein: 2.2g
carbs: 9.8g | fiber: 1.0g

Peach and Nut Cobbler

Prep time: 15 minutes | Cook time: 15 minutes | Serves 5

Cooking spray
2 pounds (907 g) peaches, peeled and roughly chopped
1 packet stevia
1 vanilla bean, split lengthwise and seeds scraped out
¼ teaspoon
cinnamon
1½ cups raw almonds
½ cup shredded unsweetened coconut
1 tablespoon coconut oil, melted
¼ teaspoon sea salt

1. Preheat the oven to 350ºF (180ºC).
2. Spray a 9-inch baking dish with cooking spray.

3. In a large saucepan over medium heat, combine the peaches, stevia, vanilla bean, and cinnamon. Stir well until the mixture comes to a boil. Remove from the heat.
4. In a food processor, combine the almonds, coconut, coconut oil, and salt. Pulse until a sticky, crumbly mixture forms.
5. Transfer the peaches to the prepared baking dish. Top with the almond-coconut mixture.
6. Bake in the preheated oven for 15 minutes, or until the top is lightly golden. Serve warm.

Per Serving (1 Cup)
calories: 241 | fat: 16.9g | protein: 6.7g
carbs: 20.9g | fiber: 5.9g

Raspberry and Walnut Energy Balls

Prep time: 5 minutes | Cook time: 0 minutes | Serves 2

½ cup raspberries
5 dates
Pinch sea salt
$1/_3$ cup walnuts
1½ cup soft-jelly coconut, shredded

1. Plug in a high-speed food processor or blender and add all the ingredients in its jar.
2. Cover the blender jar with its lid and then pulse for 40 to 60 seconds until well combined.
3. Shape the mixture into balls by using wet hands, 1 tablespoon mixture per ball, place the balls on the tray, and let them freeze for a minimum of 30 minutes.
4. Serve straight away.

Per Serving
calories: 124 | fat: 7.9g | protein: 1.0g
carbs: 11.2g | fiber: 2.1g

Walnut and Banana Spelt Bread

Prep time: 10 minutes | Cook time: 20 minutes | Serves 2

¹/₃ cup chopped walnuts
1¹/₃ cup burro banana
²/₃ cup spelt flour
¹/₈ teaspoon salt
¼ cup agave syrup
1¹/₃ tablespoons olive oil

1. Switch on the oven, then set it to 350ºF (180ºC) and let it preheat.
2. Meanwhile, place the burro banana in a medium bowl, mash it by using a fork and then stir in oil and agave syrup until combined.
3. Take a separate medium bowl, place flour in it, add salt and nuts, stir until mixed, and then stir in the burro banana mixture until smooth.
4. Pour the batter into a parchment-lined loaf pan and then bake for 20 minutes until firm and the top turn golden brown.
5. When done, let the bread cool for 10 minutes, then cut it into slices and serve.

Per Serving
calories: 187 | fat: 11.2g | protein: 1.2g
carbs: 22.1g | fiber: 1.9g

Summer Crisp

Prep time: 15 minutes | Cook time: 15 minutes | Serves 6

Cooking spray
2 cups chopped summer fruits, like strawberries and plums
1 packet stevia
1 vanilla bean, split lengthwise and seeds scraped out
1½ cups raw almonds
½ cup shredded unsweetened coconut
1 tablespoon coconut oil, melted
¼ teaspoon sea salt

1. Preheat the oven to 350ºF (180ºC).
2. Spray a 9-inch baking dish with cooking spray.
3. In a large saucepan over medium heat, combine the chopped fruits, stevia, and vanilla bean seeds. Stir until the mixture comes to a boil. Remove from the heat.
4. In a food processor, combine the almonds, coconut, coconut oil, and salt. Pulse until a sticky, crumbly mixture forms.
5. Transfer the fruits to the prepared baking dish. Top with the almond-coconut mixture.
6. Bake in the preheated oven for 15 minutes, or until the top is lightly golden.
7. Serve warm.

Per Serving (½ Cup)
calories: 241 | fat: 16.9g | protein: 6.7g
carbs: g20.7 | fiber: 5.6g

Sumptuous Melon Mix

Prep time: 15 minutes | Cook time: 0 minutes | Serves 4

½ lengthwise-cut watermelon, flesh scooped into balls, shell reserved
1 cup bite-size
honeydew melon pieces
1 cup bite-size cantaloupe pieces

1. In a large bowl, combine the watermelon balls, honeydew, and cantaloupe. Transfer the fruit to the watermelon shell and serve.
2. Use a melon baller to make the watermelon balls in a jiffy.

Per Serving (½ Cup)
calories: 32 | fat: 0.1g | protein: 0.9g
carbs: 7.5g | fiber: 0.8g

Herbed Rye Crackers

Prep time: 10 minutes | Cook time: 10 minutes | Serves 2

1 cup rye flour
1 teaspoon onion powder
½ teaspoon salt
½ teaspoon dried thyme
½ teaspoon dried basil
2 tablespoons grapeseed oil
4 tablespoons spring water

1. Switch on the oven, then set it to 400°F (205°C) and let it preheat.
2. Meanwhile, place flour in a food processor, add all the seasonings and oil, and then pulse until combined.
3. Add water, pulse until the dough comes together, and then roll it into a ½-inch thick dough.
4. Use a cookie cutter of the desired shape to cut out cookie, arrange them on a large baking sheet and then bake for 10 minutes until nicely browned.
5. Serve straight away.

Per Serving
calories: 81 | fat: 1.1g | protein: 0.7g
carbs: 16.5g | fiber: 1.6g

Walnut and Date Coconut Balls

Prep time: 5 minutes | Cook time: 0 minutes | Serves 2

¼ cup walnuts
½ cup dates, pitted
¼ cup sesame seeds
½ cup soft-jelly
coconut, grated
2 tablespoons agave syrup
¼ teaspoon sea salt

1. Plug in a high-speed food processor or blender and add all the ingredients in its jar except for sesame seeds.
2. Cover the blender jar with its lid and then pulse for 20 seconds until well combined.
3. Tip the mixture into a bowl, shape it into even size balls and then roll each ball into sesame seeds.
4. Serve straight away.

Per Serving
calories: 99 | fat: 5.3g | protein: 2.0g
carbs: 13.4g | fiber: 2.0g

Date and Raisin Oat Bites

Prep time: 3 minutes | Cook time: 10 minutes | Makes 20 bites

Nonstick cooking spray
¾ cup rolled oats
8 small dates, pitted
¼ cup unsweetened coconut flakes (optional)
¼ cup cashew
butter
1 teaspoon ground cinnamon
½ teaspoon vanilla extract
3 to 4 tablespoons water
½ cup raisins

1. Preheat the oven to 350°F (180°C). Lightly grease a baking sheet with cooking spray.
2. In a food processor, combine the oats, dates, coconut flakes (if using), cashew butter, cinnamon, and vanilla. Process until the mixture resembles coarse crumbs.
3. Add the water 1 tablespoon at a time, until a dough forms and holds together well. Transfer the mixture to a bowl and mix in the raisins until evenly distributed throughout the dough.
4. Using a mini scoop or rounded teaspoon, scoop small balls of the mixture onto the prepared baking sheet, spacing them evenly.
5. Bake for 10 minutes, or until just browned. Do not overcook.

Per Serving (2 bites)
calories: 114 | fat: 5.1g | protein: 1.9g
carbs: 16.8g | fiber: 2.1g

Strawberry Spelt Sorbet

Prep time: 10 minutes | Cook time: 0 minutes | Serves 4

2 cups strawberries
1½ teaspoons spelt flour
½ cup date sugar
2 cups spring water

1. Add date sugar, spring water, and spelt flour to a medium pot and boil on low heat for about ten minutes. Mixture should thicken, like syrup.
2. Remove the pot from the heat and allow it to cool.
3. After cooling, add puréed strawberry and mix gently.
4. Put this mixture in a container and freeze.
5. Cut it into pieces, put the sorbet into a processor and blend until smooth.
6. Put everything back in the container and leave in the refrigerator for at least 4 hours.
7. Serve and enjoy.

Per Serving
calories: 131 | fat: 0.2g | protein: 0.6g
carbs: 33.3g | fiber: 1.5g

Rice Crisp Cereal Treats

Prep time: 5 minutes | Cook time: 1 minutes | Serves 12

Cooking spray
²/₃ cup brown rice syrup
¼ cup coconut oil
1 vanilla bean, split
lengthwise and seeds scraped out
¼ teaspoon sea salt
4 cups brown rice crisp cereal

1. Spray a 9-inch baking pan with cooking spray.
2. In a medium saucepan set over medium heat, combine the brown rice syrup and coconut oil. Bring to a boil and boil for 1 minute. Stir in the vanilla bean seeds and salt.
3. In a large bowl, add the rice cereal. Pour the syrup mixture over the cereal. Mix with a wooden spoon to combine thoroughly.
4. Transfer the rice mixture to the prepared pan. Spray your hands with cooking spray and use them to press gently on the rice mixture to distribute it evenly in the pan.
5. Refrigerate for 45 minutes.
6. When ready to eat, bring to room temperature, cut into 12 bars, and serve.

Per Serving (1 Bar)
calories: 105 | fat: 4.5g | protein: 0.2g
carbs: 15.7g | fiber: 4.5g

Coconut and Fruit Ice Pops

Prep time: 5 minutes | Cook time: 0 minutes | Serves 6

1 (13-ounce / 369-g) can unsweetened coconut milk
1 packet stevia
1 vanilla bean, split
lengthwise and seeds scraped out
1½ cups chopped fresh fruit

1. In a small bowl, mix together the coconut milk, stevia, and vanilla bean seeds.
2. Evenly divide the chopped fruit among the ice pop molds. They will be partially filled.
3. Pour the coconut milk mixture over the fruit, gently shaking each mold to settle the milk.
4. Insert the ice pop handles into the molds. Freeze until completely frozen, about 2 hours.

Per Serving (1 Ice Pop)
calories: 165 | fat: 14.2g | protein: 2.6g
carbs: 7.2g | fiber: 4.1g

Coconut and Vanilla Bean Sundae

Prep time: 5 minutes | Cook time: 0 minutes | Serves 4

2 (13-ounce / 369-g) cans full-fat unsweetened coconut milk
1 cup coconut sugar
⅛ teaspoon sea salt
1 vanilla bean, split lengthwise and

seeds scraped out
Toppings of choice (bananas, shredded unsweetened coconut, chopped almonds, strawberries)

1. In a blender, blend together the coconut milk, coconut sugar, salt, and vanilla bean seeds. Transfer the mixture to a freezer-safe bowl. Freeze overnight.
2. Place two scoops of the ice cream in a small bowl. Garnish with the favorite alkaline-friendly toppings. Serve.

Per Serving
calories: 305 | fat: 22.6g | protein: 2.1g
carbs: 30.7g | fiber: 2.5g

Fig Almond Newtons

Prep time: 15 minutes | Cook time: 0 minutes | Serves 12

3 cups dried figs, stemmed
1 cup raw almonds
1 vanilla bean, split

lengthwise and seeds scraped out
½ teaspoon sea salt

1. In a food processor, combine the figs, almonds, vanilla bean seeds, and salt. Pulse until a dough forms.
2. Scoop the dough by tablespoonfuls and roll into balls by hand.
3. Refrigerate in an airtight container for up to one week.

Per Serving (1 Cookie)
calories: 171 | fat: 4.5g | protein: 3.7g
carbs: 32.1g | fiber: 5.2g

Chickpea and Peanut Butter Frosting

Prep time: 5 minutes | Cook time: 0 minutes | MAKES ¾ cup

¾ cup canned low-sodium chickpeas, drained (liquid reserved) and rinsed
2 tablespoons peanut butter or all-natural nut butter of the choice

2 tablespoons maple syrup, or 8 small dates, pitted
⅛ teaspoon sea salt
⅛ teaspoon vanilla extract
⅛ teaspoon ground cinnamon

1. In a high-speed blender, combine the chickpeas, peanut butter, maple syrup, salt, vanilla, and cinnamon. Blend until smooth and creamy.

Per Serving (2 tablespoons)
calories: 75 | fat: 2.9g | protein: 2.1g
carbs: 10.2g | fiber: 2.1g

Cashew and Banana Cream

Prep time: 3 minutes | Cook time: 0 minutes | Serves 6

4 ripe medium bananas, sliced and frozen
1 cup cashews, soaked in 2 cups water overnight, then drained
½ cup water
1 tablespoon

unsweetened carob powder, ground cinnamon, or unsweetened cocoa powder
½ teaspoon vanilla extract
⅛ teaspoon sea salt

1. In a high-speed blender, combine the frozen bananas, cashews, water, carob powder, vanilla, and salt. Blend until smooth and creamy, then serve immediately.

Per Serving (½ Cup)
calories: 200 | fat: 10.1g | protein: 5.2g
carbs: 24.8g | fiber: 3.2g

Almond Stuffed Dates with Coconut

Prep time: 10 minutes | Cook time: 0 minutes | Serves 1

4 pitted Medjool dates
4 almond halves, divided

¼ cup shredded unsweetened coconut

1. With a sharp knife, slice the dates lengthwise without cutting all the way through, so the halves are still connected.
2. Press open the dates and lay them on a flat surface. Use a rolling pin to flatten each date. Place one almond half on one side of a flattened date. Fold the other side over to enclose the almond between the date halves. Repeat with remaining dates and almonds.
3. Press each date into the coconut.
4. Eat and enjoy!

Per Serving (4 Dates)
calories: 179 | fat: 8.1g | protein: 2.1g
carbs: 27.4g | fiber: 4.2g

Banana and Blueberry Chia Pudding

Prep time: 15 minutes | Cook time: 0 minutes | Serves 2

1 cup unsweetened almond milk
4 tablespoons chia seeds
½ medium banana, sliced

2 tablespoons wild frozen blueberries
2 tablespoons sliced almonds
3 teaspoons raisins

1. Divide the almond milk and chia seeds between two 8-ounce (227-g) glass jars with tight-fitting lids or repurposed jam jars, seal tightly, and shake well.

2. Refrigerate for 2 hours, or until the mixture thickens.
3. Top each pudding with half the banana slices, 1 tablespoon the blueberries, 1 tablespoon the almonds, and 1½ teaspoons the raisins.
4. Seal the jars tightly and store in the refrigerator overnight. Enjoy one the next morning. Store the remaining jar in the refrigerator for up to 4 days.

Per Serving (1 Cup)
calories: 274 | fat: 15.1g | protein: 8.2g
carbs: 28.9g | fiber: 10.2g

Nutmeg Date Pudding

Prep time: 15 minutes | Cook time: 0 minutes | Serves 1

1¾ cups almond milk
1½ teaspoons apple cider vinegar
1¼ cups pitted Medjool dates, quartered
½ cup coconut oil
1½ teaspoons cinnamon

1½ teaspoons ginger
¼ teaspoon freshly grated whole nutmeg
1 vanilla bean, split lengthwise and seeds scraped out
1 teaspoon sea salt

1. In a medium bowl, combine the almond milk and cider vinegar. Let sit for 10 minutes until the milk curdles.
2. In a blender, add the dates, coconut oil, cinnamon, ginger, nutmeg, vanilla bean seeds, and sea salt. Top with the milk mixture. Process until smooth.
3. Pour the pudding into an airtight container and chill, or serve immediately.

Per Serving
calories: 305 | fat: 19.7g | protein: 3.2g
carbs: 32.7g | fiber: 3.7g

Apple Crumble

Prep time: 5 minutes | Cook time: 20 to 25 minutes | Serves 4

4 small apples
¼ cup gluten-free rolled oats
¼ cup unsweetened shredded coconut
3 or 4 small dates, pitted
1 teaspoon coconut oil

1 teaspoon maple syrup
⅛ teaspoon ground cinnamon
⅛ teaspoon vanilla extract
⅛ teaspoon sea salt

1. Preheat the oven to 400ºF (205ºC).
2. Core each apple, but leave the bottom intact to form a cup. Place each apple on a 8-inch square of aluminum foil.
3. In a high-speed blender or food processor, combine the oats, shredded coconut, dates, coconut oil, maple syrup, cinnamon, vanilla, and salt and blend until well combined.
4. Stuff each apple with approximately 2 tablespoons the oat mixture.
5. Wrap the foil around each apple, leaving a bit of the top exposed, and place the apples on a baking sheet. Bake for 20 to 25 minutes, until the apples are soft and the filling is golden.

Per Serving (1 Apple)
calories: 163 | fat: 4.9g | protein: 1.1g | carbs: 32.2g | fiber: 5.9g

Banana and Blueberry Soft Serve

Prep time: 5 minutes | Cook time: 0 minutes | Serves 2

1 small ripe banana
1 cup frozen wild blueberries

1 teaspoon freshly squeezed lemon juice

1. In a high-speed blender or food processor, combine banana, blueberries, and lemon juice. Blend until creamy and smooth. Enjoy immediately.

Per Serving (½ Cup)
calories: 82 | fat: 1.0g | protein: 1.1g | carbs: 19.9g | fiber: 3.2g

Raisin Cookies with Cashew-Date Frosting

Prep time: 5 to 7 minutes | Cook time: 12 minutes | Makes 12 cookies

For The Raisin Cookies:

10 small dates, pitted
¼ cup cashew butter
¼ cup unsweetened finely shredded coconut
¼ cup almond meal
1 medium egg
1 tablespoon coconut oil
¼ teaspoon vanilla extract

¼ teaspoon ground cinnamon
⅛ teaspoon sea salt
¾ cup rolled oats
¼ cup brown rice flour
½ teaspoon baking soda
¼ cup golden raisins
3 tablespoons chopped walnuts
2 tablespoons shredded carrot

For The Cashew-Date Frosting:

1 cup cashews, soaked in water overnight, then drained
8 small dates, pitted
½ cup water
¼ cup unsweetened shredded coconut

1 to 2 teaspoons freshly squeezed lemon juice (optional)
¼ teaspoon vanilla extract
⅛ teaspoon sea salt

To Make the Raisin Cookies

1. Preheat the oven to 375ºF (190ºC). Line a baking sheet with parchment paper.
2. In a food processor, combine the dates, cashew butter, shredded coconut, almond meal, egg, coconut oil, vanilla, cinnamon, and salt. Blend until smooth and well combined.
3. In a medium bowl, combine the oats, brown rice flour, and baking soda. Add the wet ingredients and stir to combine well.
4. Fold in the raisins, walnuts, and carrot.
5. Scoop the mixture into 1½-inch balls and place them on the prepared baking sheet, spacing them evenly. Bake for 12 minutes, or until a toothpick inserted into the center of a cookie comes out clean. Let cool completely.

To make the Cashew-Date Frosting

1. In a high-speed blender, combine the cashews, dates, water, shredded coconut, lemon juice (if using), vanilla, and salt. Blend until well combined, with date specks sprinkled throughout.
2. Frost each cookie with about 1 rounded teaspoon the cashew-date frosting.

Per Serving (1 Cookie)
calories: 165 | fat: 9.1g | protein: 4.2g | carbs: 20.1g | fiber: 3.1g

Chapter 11: Smoothies

Kale, Apple, and Banana Smoothie

Prep time: 5 minutes | Cook time: 0 minutes | Serves 2

1 cup kale	½ of a burro
½ apple, cored, sliced	banana
1 teaspoon sea moss	1 teaspoon bromide plus powder

1. Plug in a high-speed food processor or blender and add all the ingredients in its jar.
2. Cover the blender jar with its lid and then pulse for 40 to 60 seconds until smooth.
3. Divide the drink between two glasses and then serve.

Per Serving
calories: 116 | fat: 0.6g | protein: 2.1g
carbs: 28.1g | fiber: 1.9g

Watermelon and Strawberry Smoothie

Prep time: 5 minutes | Cook time: 0 minutes | Serves 1

1 cup watermelon chunks	1 tablespoon date syrup
1 cup strawberries	1 cup coconut water

1. Combine all ingredients in the blender.
2. Blend until smooth.
3. Serve and enjoy.

Per Serving
calories: 190 | fat: 1.2g | protein: 3.6g
carbs: 45.0g | fiber: 6.1g

Banana, Date and Walnut Smoothie

Prep time: 5 minutes | Cook time: 0 minutes | Serves 2

1 burro banana, peeled	homemade
4 dates, pitted, chopped	6 tablespoons walnut
1 cup walnut milk,	1 cup soft-jelly coconut water

1. Plug in a high-speed food processor or blender and add all the ingredients in its jar.
2. Cover the blender jar with its lid and then pulse for 40 to 60 seconds until smooth.
3. Divide the drink between two glasses and then serve.

Per Serving
calories: 200 | fat: 5.1g | protein: 5.9g
carbs: 34.8g | fiber: 3.4g

Summer Fruity Smoothie

Prep time: 10 minutes | Cook time: 0 minutes | Serves 2

1 chopped seville orange	½ chopped burro banana or 1 baby
1 cup diced mango	banana
1 cup raspberries	1 cup water

1. Combine all ingredients into the blender.
2. Blend until smooth.
3. Serve and enjoy.

Per Serving
calories: 139 | fat: 0.9g | protein: 2.4g
carbs: 34.1g | fiber: 7.7g

Apple and Kale Smoothie

Prep time: 5 minutes | Cook time: 0 minutes | Serves 2

1 apple, peeled, cored, chopped
2 cups kale leaves
1 teaspoon key lime juice
1¼ cups orange juice
Pinch cayenne pepper

1. Plug in a high-speed food processor or blender and add all the ingredients in its jar.
2. Cover the blender jar with its lid and then pulse for 40 to 60 seconds until smooth.
3. Divide the drink between two glasses and then serve.

Per Serving
calories: 189 | fat: 1.1g | protein: 4.5g
carbs: 50.1g | fiber: 13.9g

Arugula, Banana, and Apple Smoothie

Prep time: 5 minutes | Cook time: 0 minutes | Serves 2

2 cups arugula
1 burro banana, peeled
2 apples, cored
2 cups soft-jelly coconut water
4 tablespoons key lime juice

1. Plug in a high-speed food processor or blender and add all the ingredients in its jar.
2. Cover the blender jar with its lid and then pulse for 40 to 60 seconds until smooth.
3. Divide the drink between two glasses and then serve.

Per Serving
calories: 181 | fat: 0g | protein: 0g
carbs: 44.8g | fiber: 7.9g

Blueberry, Watercress, and Dandelion Smoothie

Prep time: 10 minutes | Cook time: 0 minutes | Serves 2

½ cup blueberries
1 small bunch watercress
6 medium dates
1 large bunch dandelion greens
3 chopped baby bananas
1 thumb chopped ginger (optional)
1 tablespoon burdock root powder
2 cups coconut water
¼ cup lime juice

1. Prepare and place all ingredients into the blender.
2. Blend for two minutes until smooth.
3. Serve it and enjoy.

Per Serving
calories: 320 | fat: 1.9g | protein: 7.2g
carbs: 77.9g | fiber: 13.0g

Banana and Rainbow Chard Smoothie

Prep time: 5 minutes | Cook time: 0 minutes | Serves 1 to 2

1½ cups coconut milk (boxed)
½ to 1 banana, roughly chopped
½ cup chopped rainbow or red chard
2 tablespoons almond butter
2 tablespoons hemp seeds
5 to 7 ice cubes (optional)

1. In a blender, blend to combine the coconut milk, banana, chard, almond butter, hemp seeds, and ice (if using) until creamy and smooth.
2. Pour into 1 large or 2 small glasses and enjoy.

Per Serving
calories: 511 | fat: 49.7g | protein: 9.1g
carbs: 16.6g | fiber: 3.3g

Avocado, Pear, and Cucumber Smoothie

Prep time: 10 minutes | Cook time: 0 minutes | Serves 1

¼ avocado
1 chopped pear
½ chopped cucumber
1 handful of romaine lettuce
Date sugar (optional)
1 handful of watercress
½ cup spring water

1. Prepare and place all ingredients in the blender.
2. Blend for one minute until smooth.
3. Serve and enjoy.

Per Serving
calories: 186 | fat: 8.0g | protein: 4.1g carbs: 30.1g | fiber: 10.2g

Kale and Peach Protein Smoothie

Prep time: 5 minutes | Cook time: 0 minutes | Serves 1 to 2

1½ cups coconut milk (boxed)
2 romaine lettuce leaves
1 kale stalk, stemmed
1 peach, roughly chopped
½ to 1 banana, roughly chopped
5 tablespoons pumpkin protein powder
5 to 7 ice cubes (optional)

1. In a blender, blend to combine the coconut milk, lettuce, kale, peach, banana, pumpkin protein powder, and ice (if using) until smooth.
2. Pour into 1 large or 2 small glasses and enjoy.

Per Serving
calories: 521 | fat: 41.5g | protein: 18.6g carbs: 27.2g | fiber: 5.5g

Watermelon and Dark Cherry Smoothie

Prep time: 5 minutes | Cook time: 0 minutes | Serves 1 to 2

2 cups cubed watermelon
10 pitted dark sweet cherries
1 cup coconut milk (boxed)
1 tablespoon brown rice syrup
1 tablespoon freshly squeezed lime juice
5 to 7 ice cubes (optional)

1. In a blender, blend to combine the water-melon, cherries, coconut milk, brown rice syrup, lime juice, and ice (if using) until smooth.
2. Pour into 1 large or 2 small glasses and enjoy.

Per Serving
calories: 177 | fat: 4.3g | protein: 5.3g carbs: 32.4g | fiber: 1.5g

Currant and Peach Smoothie

Prep time: 5 minutes | Cook time: 0 minutes | Serves 1

½ cup red currants
2 quartered peaches
1 tablespoon agave syrup
1 teaspoon bromide plus powder
1 cup coconut milk
½ cup ice

1. Prepare all ingredients except Ice and add them to a blender.
2. Blend until smooth.
3. Add Ice and blend once more.
4. Serve and enjoy.

Per Serving
calories: 397 | fat: 11.3g | protein: 12.3g carbs: 66.8g | fiber: 6.9g

Sumptuous Vegetable Smoothie

Prep time: 15 minutes | Cook time: 0 minutes | Serves 1

½ carrot, peeled and chopped
½ celery stalk, chopped
¼ onion, chopped
1 medium tomato, chopped
2 cups spinach
½ red bell pepper, seeded and chopped
½ cucumber, peeled and chopped
¼ cup fresh cilantro, stemmed
¼ teaspoon cumin
¼ teaspoon garlic powder
Pinch sea salt
Fresh tomato juice, as needed

1. In a blender, place the carrot, celery, onion, tomato, spinach, red bell pepper, cucumber, cilantro, cumin, garlic powder, and salt.
2. Pulse until the desired consistency.
3. If the mixture is too thick, slowly add the tomato juice until you have the desired consistency.
4. Serve in a tall glass.

Per Serving
calories: 103 | fat: 0.9g | protein: 5.0g carbs: 21.6g | fiber: 6.4g

Lush Mango and Banana Smoothie

Prep time: 10 minutes | Cook time: 0 minutes | Serves 2

2 fresh chopped mangoes
1 cup frozen chopped mangoes
3 frozen quartered burro bananas

1. Prepare and place all ingredients in the blender.
2. Blend for one minute until smooth.
3. Serve and enjoy.

Per Serving
calories: 409 | fat: 2.2g | protein: 5.4g carbs: 103.1g | fiber: 11.3g

Avocado, Cucumber, and Blueberry Smoothie

Prep time: 5 minutes | Cook time: 0 minutes | Serves 1 to 2

1½ cups coconut milk (boxed)
1 avocado, roughly chopped
1 cucumber, peeled and roughly chopped
½ to 1 banana, roughly chopped
1 cup fresh or frozen blueberries
5 to 7 ice cubes (optional)

1. In a blender, blend to combine the coconut milk, avocado, cucumber, banana, blueberries, and ice (if using) until creamy and smooth.
2. Pour into 1 large or 2 small glasses and enjoy.

Per Serving
calories: 593 | fat: 51.7g | protein: 7.1g carbs: 35.0g | fiber: 10.3g

Kiwi and Mango Smoothie

Prep time: 5 minutes | Cook time: 0 minutes | Serves 1 to 2

1½ cups coconut milk (boxed)
½ cup chopped mango
1 kiwi, peeled and chopped
¼ cup raw cashews
5 to 7 ice cubes (optional)

1. In a high-speed blender, blend to combine the coconut milk, mango, kiwi, cashews, and ice (if using) until smooth.
2. Pour into 1 large or 2 small glasses and enjoy.

Per Serving
calories: 560 | fat: 51.5g | protein: 7.6g carbs: 27.3g | fiber: 7.1g

Kiwi and Blueberry Smoothie

Prep time: 5 minutes | Cook time: 0 minutes | Serves 1 to 2

1½ cups almond milk
1 kiwi, peeled and chopped
1 cup fresh or

frozen blueberries
2 tablespoons hemp seeds
5 to 7 ice cubes (optional)

1. In a blender, blend to combine the almond milk, kiwi, blueberries, hemp seeds, and ice (if using) until smooth.
2. Pour into 1 large or 2 small glasses and enjoy.

Per Serving
calories: 204 | fat: 7.8g | protein: 3.8g
carbs: 33.5g | fiber: 5.6g

Apple and Ginger Green Smoothie

Prep time: 5 minutes | Cook time: 0 minutes | Serves 1 to 2

1½ cups coconut milk (boxed)
2 stalks kale, stemmed and roughly chopped
2 stalks romaine lettuce, roughly chopped
½ celery stalk, roughly chopped

1 apple, cored and roughly chopped
1 tablespoon freshly squeezed lemon juice
¼- to ½-inch piece ginger root, peeled and chopped
5 to 7 ice cubes (optional)

1. In a high-speed blender, blend to combine the coconut milk, kale, romaine, celery, apple, lemon juice, ginger, and ice (if using) until smooth.
2. Pour into 1 large or 2 small glasses and enjoy.

Per Serving
calories: 404 | fat: 36.7g | protein: 5.3g
carbs: 21.8g | fiber: 3.9g

Blackberry, Avocado, and Banana Smoothie

Prep time: 5 minutes | Cook time: 0 minutes | Serves 1 to 2

1½ cups coconut milk
1 cup blackberries
½ avocado, roughly

chopped
½ banana, roughly chopped

1. In a blender, blend to combine the coconut milk, blackberries, avocado, and banana until creamy and smooth.
2. Pour into 1 large or 2 small glasses and enjoy.

Per Serving
calories: 472 | fat: 44.0g | protein: 5.8g
carbs: 22.7g | fiber: 7.9g

Orange and Banana Smoothie

Prep time: 2 minutes | Cook time: 0 minutes | Serves 1

6 ounces (170 g) freshly squeezed orange juice
1 ounce (28 g) unsweetened coconut milk
1 medium frozen

banana, cut into chunks
1 vanilla bean, split lengthwise and seeds scraped out
1 packet stevia (optional)

1. In a blender, add the orange juice, coconut milk, banana, vanilla bean seeds, and stevia (if using).
2. Process until smooth.
3. Serve in a tall glass.

Per Serving
calories: 183 | fat: 0.4g | protein: 2.4g
carbs: 44.1g | fiber: 3.7g

Pumpkin and Banana Smoothie

Prep time: 2 minutes | Cook time: 0 minutes | Serves 1

½ cup pumpkin purée
1 banana, frozen
1 cup unsweetened coconut milk
1 vanilla bean, split lengthwise and
seeds scraped out
¼ teaspoon cinnamon
⅛ teaspoon nutmeg
⅛ teaspoon allspice
½ cup ice cubes

1. In a blender, add the pumpkin, banana, coconut milk, vanilla bean seeds, cinnamon, nutmeg, allspice, and ice.
2. Process until smooth.
3. Serve in a tall glass.

Per Serving
calories: 241 | fat: 5.6g | protein: 3.5g carbs: 47.7g | fiber: 7.7g

Kale, Avocado, and Banana Smoothie

Prep time: 5 minutes | Cook time: 0 minutes | Serves 1 to 2

1½ cups almond milk
2 kale stalks, stemmed
½ avocado, roughly
chopped
½ banana, roughly chopped
1 tablespoon hemp seeds

1. In a blender, blend to combine the almond milk, kale, avocado, banana, and hemp seeds until creamy and smooth.
2. Pour into 1 large or 2 small glasses and enjoy.

Per Serving
calories: 236 | fat: 12.2g | protein: 4.6g carbs: 31.3g | fiber: 6.3g

Raspberry and Banana Smoothie

Prep time: 5 minutes | Cook time: 0 minutes | Serves 1 to 2

1½ cups coconut milk (boxed)
1 cup raspberries
½ banana
1 teaspoon freshly squeezed lime juice
5 to 7 ice cubes (optional)
Fresh mint leaves, for garnish (optional)

1. In a blender, blend to combine the coconut milk, raspberries, banana, lime juice, and mint leaves (if using) until well combined and smooth.
2. Pour into 1 or 2 glasses and enjoy.

Per Serving
calories: 473 | fat: 43.4g | protein: 5.2g carbs: 24.3g | fiber: 8.7g

Asian Pear and Chinese Cabbage Smoothie

Prep time: 5 minutes | Cook time: 0 minutes | Serves 1

1 cup unsweetened, lime-flavored sparkling water
1 Asian pear, peeled and sliced
½ cup Chinese
cabbage
1 teaspoon grated fresh ginger
1 packet stevia
½ cup ice cubes

1. In the blender, place the sparkling water, pear, cabbage, ginger, stevia, and ice.
2. Carefully process, covered, until blended.
3. Serve in a tall glass.

Per Serving
calories: 86 | fat: 0.3g | protein: 1.1g carbs: 22.4g | fiber: 4.5g

Berry Pumpkin Protein Smoothie

Prep time: 5 minutes | Cook time: 0 minutes | Serves 1 to 2

1½ cups coconut milk (boxed)
⅓ cup raspberries
⅓ cup blueberries
⅓ cup blackberries
3 tablespoons 100% pumpkin protein powder

1. In a blender, blend to combine the coconut milk, raspberries, blueberries, blackberries, and pumpkin protein powder until well combined and smooth.

Per Serving
calories: 433 | fat: 39.3g | protein: 11.7g
carbs: 15.3g | fiber: 4.0g

Burro Banana, Kale, and Pear Smoothie

Prep time: 5 minutes | Cook time: 0 minutes | Serves 2

1 burro banana, peeled
2 cups chopped kale
1 pear, diced
1 cup soft-jelly coconut water

1. Plug in a high-speed food processor or blender and add all the ingredients in its jar.
2. Cover the blender jar with its lid and then pulse for 40 to 60 seconds until smooth.
3. Divide the drink between two glasses and then serve.

Per Serving
calories: 91 | fat: 0g | protein: 1.0g
carbs: 24.1g | fiber: 3.2g

Pineapple Smoothie

Prep time: 2 minutes | Cook time: 0 minutes | Serves 1

½ cup unsweetened coconut milk
2½ cups fresh pineapple chunks
(or canned unsweetened)
1 cup ice cubes

1. To a blender, add the coconut milk, pineapple, and ice.
2. Blend until smooth.
3. Serve in a tall glass.

Per Serving
calories: 176 | fat: 3.3g | protein: 1.6g
carbs: 38.8g | fiber: 3.7g

Banana and Almond Smoothie

Prep time: 2 minutes | Cook time: 0 minutes | Serves 1

1 cup filtered water
1 medium banana, peeled
¼ cup raw almonds
½ teaspoon cinnamon
¼ teaspoon nutmeg
1 whole vanilla bean, split lengthwise and seeds scraped out
½ cup ice cubes

1. To a blender, add the water, banana, almonds, cinnamon, nutmeg, vanilla bean seeds, and ice.
2. Blend until smooth.
3. Serve in a tall glass.

Per Serving
calories: 255 | fat: 12.2g | protein: 6.4g
carbs: 33.5g | fiber: 7.1g

Raspberry, Mango, and Papaya Smoothie

Prep time: 2 minutes | Cook time: 0 minutes | Serves 1

¼ cup raspberries
¾ cup frozen mango pieces
½ medium papaya, seeds removed and chopped

1. In a blender, add the raspberries, mango, and papaya.
2. Process until smooth.
3. Serve in a tall glass.

Per Serving
calories: 154 | fat: 0.1g | protein: 2.2g
carbs: 39.8g | fiber: 6.6g

Spinach and Pineapple Mint Smoothie

Prep time: 2 minutes | Cook time: 0 minutes | Serves 1

1 cup spinach
1 cup unsweetened coconut water
2 cups pineapple
2 tablespoons fresh mint leaves
Juice of ½ lime

1. In a blender, add the spinach, coconut water, pineapple, mint leaves, and lime juice.
2. Process until smooth.
3. Serve in a tall glass.

Per Serving
calories: 242 | fat: 1.6g | protein: 2.5g
carbs: 60.5g | fiber: 5.2g

Dark Cherry and Chocolate Smoothie

Prep time: 2 minutes | Cook time: 0 minutes | Serves 1

½ cup frozen dark cherries
¾ cup filtered water
1 teaspoon Dutch-
processed cocoa powder
1 packet stevia (optional)

1. In a blender, add the cherries, water, cocoa powder, and stevia (if using).
2. Process until smooth.
3. Serve in a tall glass.

Per Serving
calories: 61 | fat: 0.5g | protein: 0.6g
carbs: 13.3g | fiber: 1.9g

Spinach and Peach Smoothie

Prep time: 2 minutes | Cook time: 0 minutes | Serves 1

1 cup spinach
1 cup unsweetened coconut milk
1 cup frozen sliced peaches

1. In a blender, add the spinach, coconut milk, and peaches.
2. Process until smooth.
3. Serve in a tall glass.

Per Serving
calories: 231 | fat: 6.1g | protein: 5.0g
carbs: 43.6g | fiber: 5.7g

Kale and Banana Smoothie

Prep time: 2 minutes | Cook time: 0 minutes | Serves 1

½ cup kale
1 medium banana, extra ripe
1 cup fresh pineapple juice

½ cup ice cubes
1 packet stevia (optional)

1. In a blender, place the kale, banana, pineapple juice, ice, and stevia (if using).
2. Process until smooth.
3. Serve in a tall glass.

Per Serving
calories: 255 | fat: 0.1g | protein: 3.2g | carbs: 62.6g | fiber: 4.4g

Fruit and Kale Smoothie

Prep time: 10 minutes | Cook time: 0 minutes | Serves 1

1 orange, peeled and seeded
1 medium peach, peeled and sliced

1 cup chopped kale
8 ounces (227 g) filtered water

1. In a blender, place the orange, peach, kale, and water.
2. Process until smooth.
3. Serve in a tall glass.

Per Serving
calories: 159 | fat: 0.1g | protein: 4.5g | carbs: 38.1g | fiber: 7.1g

Lemon and Ginger Smoothie

Prep time: 2 minutes | Cook time: 0 minutes | Serves 1

1 cup warm water
Juice of 1 lemon
¼ teaspoon grated fresh ginger

1 garlic clove, peeled
½ teaspoon sesame oil
¼ teaspoon sea salt

1. In a blender, add the water, lemon juice, ginger, garlic, sesame oil, and salt.
2. Pulse until the desired consistency.
3. Serve in a tall glass.

Per Serving
calories: 36 | fat: 2.4g | protein: 0.4g | carbs: 4.4g | fiber: 0.2g

Chapter 12: Herbal Tea

Dandelion and Prodigiosa Cleansing Tea

Prep time: 5 minutes | Cook time: 0 minutes | Serves 1

1 teaspoon dandelion root powder

1 teaspoon Prodigiosa powder
1 cup spring water

1. Place all ingredients in a tea kettle
2. Boil for 10 minutes, remove from heat, cover and leave for an additional 10 minutes.
3. Drain and serve

Per Serving
calories: 20 | fat: 0.1g | protein: 0.1g
carbs: 5.1g | fiber: 0.2g

Cascara and Cahparral Cleansing Tea

Prep time: 5 minutes | Cook time: 0 minutes | Serves 1

1 teaspoon Cascara powder
1 teaspoon

Cahparral
1 cup spring water

1. Place all ingredients in a tea kettle
2. Boil for 10 minutes, remove from heat, cover and leave for an additional 10 minutes.
3. Drain and serve

Per Serving
calories: 23 | fat: 0.3g | protein: 0.3g
carbs: 5.5g | fiber: 1.1g

Dandelion and Burdock Cleansing Tea

Prep time: 5 minutes | Cook time: 0 minutes | Serves 1

1 teaspoon dandelion root powder

1 teaspoon burdock root powder
1 cup spring water

1. Place all ingredients in a tea kettle.
2. Boil for 10 minutes, remove from heat, cover and leave for an additional 10 minutes.
3. Drain and serve

Per Serving
calories: 6 | fat: 0g | protein: 0.1g
carbs: 1.5g | fiber: 0.3g

Prodigiosa and Burdock Cleansing Tea

Prep time: 5 minutes | Cook time: 0 minutes | Serves 1

1 teaspoon Prodigiosa powder
1 teaspoon burdock

root powder
1 cup spring water

1. Place all ingredients in a tea kettle
2. Boil for 10 minutes, remove from heat, cover and leave for an additional 10 minutes.
3. Drain and serve

Per Serving
calories: 20 | fat: 0.1g | protein: 0.1g
carbs: 5.1g | fiber: 0.2g

Cascara and Rhubard Cleansing Tea

Prep time: 5 minutes | Cook time: 0 minutes | Serves 1

1 teaspoon Cascara powder
1 teaspoon Rhubard

root powder
1 cup spring water

1. Place all ingredients in a tea kettle
2. Boil for 10 minutes, remove from heat, cover and leave for an additional 10 minutes.
3. Drain and serve

Per Serving
calories: 11 | fat: 0.4g | protein: 0.5g
carbs: 2.1g | fiber: 1.1g

Chapter 13: Staples

Sweet Barbecue Sauce

Prep time: 15 minutes | Cook time: 25 minutes | Makes 1 cup

6 quartered plum tomatoes
¼ cup chopped white onions
¼ cup date sugar
2 teaspoons pure sea salt
2 tablespoons agave syrup
¼ teaspoon cayenne pepper
2 teaspoons onion powder
½ teaspoon ground ginger
⅛ teaspoon cloves

1. Add all ingredients, excluding date sugar, to a blender and blend them thoroughly.
2. Pour mixture into a saucepan and add date sugar.
3. Cook over medium heat, stirring occasionally to prevent sticking until boiling.
4. Reduce heat to a simmer. Cover the saucepan with a lid and cook for 15 minutes, stirring from time to time.
5. Use an immersion blender to blend the sauce until it is smooth.
6. Continue to cook at low heat until sauce thickens (about 10 minutes).
7. Allow mixture to cool before using.
8. Serve and enjoy.

Per Serving
calories: 413 | fat: 1.0g | protein: 4.3g
carbs: 102.9g | fiber: 6.9g

Tomato Sauce

Prep time: 10 minutes | Cook time: 0 minutes | Makes 1 cup

5 Roma tomatoes
1 pinch of basil
1 teaspoon oregano
1 teaspoon onion powder
2 tablespoons minced onion
2 tablespoons agave syrup
1 teaspoon pure sea salt
2 tablespoons grape seed oil

1. Make an X cut on the bottom of the Roma tomatoes and place them into a pot of boiling water for just 1 minute.
2. Remove the tomatoes from the water with a spoon and shock them, placing them in cold water for 30 seconds.
3. Take them out and immediately peel with the fingers or a knife.
4. Put all the ingredients into a blender or a food processor and blend for 1 minute until smooth.
5. Serve and enjoy.

Per Serving
calories: 474 | fat: 28.5g | protein: 6.0g
carbs: 55.2g | fiber: 8.5g

Chimichurri

Prep time: 5 minutes | Cook time: 0 minutes | Makes ½ cup

2 handfuls fresh parsley leaves
1 handful fresh cilantro leaves
3 garlic cloves
¼ cup avocado oil
2 tablespoons apple cider vinegar
1 teaspoon red pepper flakes
¼ teaspoon sea salt
½ teaspoon freshly ground black pepper

1. In a blender, blend together the parsley, cilantro, garlic, avocado oil, vinegar, red pepper flakes, salt, and pepper until well combined. Adjust seasonings, if necessary.
2. Store in an airtight container in the refrigerator.

Per Serving (½ Cup)
calories: 267 | fat: 27.7g | protein: 1.5g
carbs: 4.7g | fiber: 1.6g

Hawaiian Mango and Pineapple Salsa

Prep time: 20 minutes | Cook time: 0 minutes | Serves 6

4 fully ripened tomatoes, diced
½ sweet onion (Maui or Vidalia), diced
½ cup diced fresh mango
½ cup diced pineapple
¼ cup apple cider vinegar
½ teaspoon sea salt

1. In a large airtight container, mix together the tomatoes, onion, mango, pineapple, cider vinegar, and salt. Cover and chill for 15 minutes so the flavors blend before serving.

Per Serving (¼ Cup)
calories: 50 | fat: 0.3g | protein: 1.0g
carbs: 5.4g | fiber: 1.5g

Pico de Gallo

Prep time: 20 minutes | Cook time: 0 minutes | Serves 6

4 fully ripened tomatoes, diced
½ sweet onion (Maui or Vidalia), diced
1 tablespoon toasted cumin seeds
¼ cup chopped fresh cilantro
¼ cup apple cider vinegar
½ teaspoon sea salt

1. In a large airtight container, mix together the tomatoes, onion, cumin seeds, cilantro, cider vinegar, and salt. Cover and chill for 15 minutes so the flavors blend before serving.

Per Serving (¼ Cup)
calories: 26 | fat: 0.5g | protein: 1.6g
carbs: 4.5g | fiber: 1.3g

Whipped Vanilla Coconut Cream

Prep time: 15 minutes | Cook time: 0 minutes | Serves 8

1 (13-ounce / 369-g) can full-fat unsweetened coconut milk, chilled
1 packet stevia
1 vanilla bean, split lengthwise and seeds scraped out

1. Open the can of coconut milk. Use a spoon to scoop out the thick layer of coconut milk fat. Place it into a large bowl. Using a whisk or hand mixer, beat just as you would regular whipping cream, until fluffy.
2. Add the stevia and vanilla bean seeds and whip for another minute or so.
3. Use immediately or store covered in the refrigerator for one to two days.

Per Serving (¼ Cup)
calories: 200 | fat: 21.1g | protein: 1.9g
carbs: 2.9g | fiber: 0.2g

Spicy Barbecue Sauce

Prep time: 5 minutes | Cook time: 25 minutes | Serves 6

2 cups water
1 onion, chopped
1 (8-ounce / 227-g) can tomato sauce
¼ cup apple cider vinegar
2 teaspoons paprika
2 teaspoons chili powder
1 packet stevia

1. In a medium saucepan, combine the water, onion, tomato sauce, cider vinegar, paprika, chili powder, and stevia. Bring the ingredients to a full boil.
2. Reduce the heat and simmer for 20 minutes.
3. Serve immediately, or cool and refrigerate in an airtight container.

Per Serving (2 Tablespoons)
calories: 37 | fat: 0.9g | protein: 1.4g
carbs: 6.9g | fiber: 2.4g

Basil Avocado Sauce

Prep time: 10 minutes | Cook time: 0 minutes | Makes 1 cup

1 ripe avocado
1 pinch basil
½ teaspoon oregano
½ teaspoon onion powder
2 tablespoons minced onion
½ teaspoon pure sea salt

1. Cut the avocado in half, peel it, and remove the seed.
2. Chop it into small pieces and throw into a food processor.
3. Add all other ingredients and blend for 2 to 3 minutes until smooth.
4. Serve and enjoy.

Per Serving
calories: 335 | fat: 29.5g | protein: 4.4g
carbs: 20.3g | fiber: 14.2g

Alkaline Fruit Jam

Prep time: 5 minutes | Cook time: 0 minutes | Makes 1 cup

1½ cups alkaline fruit (chopped mango, blueberries, chopped strawberries, blackberries, etc.)
¼ cup chia seeds
1 to 2 tablespoons unrefined whole cane sugar, such as Sucanat

1. In a food processor, process the fruit, chia seeds, and sugar until well blended. Adjust the sweetener, if necessary.
2. Store extra chia jam in an airtight container in the refrigerator.

Per Serving
calories: 463 | fat: 18.4g | protein: 11.4g
carbs: 71.4g | fiber: 23.5g

Shallot-Onion Sauce

Prep time: 15 minutes | Cook time: 0 minutes | Makes 1 cup

¼ cup diced shallots
1 tablespoon onion powder
¼ teaspoon dill
½ teaspoon ginger
½ teaspoon pure sea salt
1 cup grape seed oil

1. Find a glass jar with a lid.
2. Put all ingredients for the sauce in the jar and shake them well.
3. Place the sauce mixture in the refrigerator for at least 1 hour.
4. Serve and enjoy.

Per Serving
calories: 1962 | fat: 217.8g | protein: 1.3g
carbs: 8.8g | fiber: 1.7g

Coconut Sweet Sauce

Prep time: 5 minutes | Cook time: 10 minutes | Serves 6

1 tablespoon coconut oil
3 tablespoons coconut flour
2¼ cups almond milk
1 teaspoon sea salt
1 teaspoon garlic powder
1 teaspoon onion powder

1. In a saucepan set over medium heat, gently heat the coconut oil. Don't let it get too hot or the flour will instantly burn.
2. Add the coconut flour and whisk to make a thick paste.
3. Add the almond milk and bring to a boil. Boil for 2 minutes, then lower heat.
4. Add the salt, garlic powder, and onion powder. Simmer until thickened.
5. Serve warm.

Per Serving (½ Cup)
calories: 85 | fat: 4.2g | protein: 3.6g
carbs: 8.2g | fiber: 0.6g

Cinnamon Apple Butter

Prep time: 10 minutes | Cook time: 3 hours | Serves 24

4 pounds (1.8 kg) apples, peeled, cored, and chopped
2 cups fresh apple juice
1 tablespoon freshly squeezed lemon juice
2 packets stevia
1 teaspoon cinnamon
1 vanilla bean, split lengthwise and seeds scraped out
Pinch ground cloves

1. In a large pot, combine the apples, apple juice, and lemon juice. Bring to a simmer and cook for 1 hour, until soft. Remove from the heat and cool slightly.

2. Using an immersion blender (or the regular blender in batches), purée the apples until smooth.
3. Add the stevia, cinnamon, vanilla bean seeds, and cloves to the apples. Return the pot to the heat and cook for an additional 2 hours, stirring frequently.
4. Cool the apple butter. Transfer to an airtight container and refrigerate.

Per Serving (2 Tablespoons)
calories: 50 | fat: 0.3g | protein: 0.3g
carbs: 13.0g | fiber: 2.0g

Classic Guacamole

Prep time: 15 minutes | Cook time: 0 minutes | Makes 2 cups

1 minced Roma tomato
2 avocados
½ cup chopped cilantro
½ cup minced red onion
½ teaspoon
cayenne powder
½ teaspoon onion powder
½ teaspoon pure sea salt
Juice from a half of lime

1. Cut the avocados in half, peel, and remove the seeds.
2. Chop into small pieces and put them in a medium bowl.
3. Add all other ingredients, excluding the Roma tomato, to the bowl.
4. Using a masher, mix together until smooth.
5. Add the minced Roma tomato to the mixture and mix well.
6. Serve and enjoy.

Per Serving (1 Cup)
calories: 349 | fat: 29.7g | protein: 5.2g
carbs: 23.4g | fiber: 14.8g

Tzatziki Sauce

Prep time: 5 minutes | Cook time: 0 minutes | Makes 2 cups

1 cup raw cashews
½ cup water
1 cucumber, peeled and sliced
2 garlic cloves
4 tablespoons freshly squeezed lemon juice

2 tablespoons tahini
3 tablespoons chopped fresh dill, divided
1 tablespoon chopped fresh parsley leaves
½ to ¾ teaspoon sea salt
⅛ teaspoon freshly ground black pepper

1. In a high-speed blender, blend together the cashews, water, cucumber, garlic, lemon juice, tahini, 1 tablespoon dill, and the parsley, salt, and pepper until creamy and smooth. Adjust the seasonings, if necessary.
2. Transfer to a small bowl, and stir in the remaining 2 tablespoons the dill.
3. Store in an airtight container in the refrigerator.

Per Serving (1 Cup)
calories: 537 | fat: 41.5g | protein: 15.6g | carbs: 36.6g | fiber: 6.5g

Enchilada Sauce

Prep time: 5 minutes | Cook time: 26 minutes | Serves 8

2 tablespoons coconut oil
2 tablespoons coconut flour
2 tablespoons chili powder
2 cups water
1 (8-ounce / 227-g) can tomato paste

1 teaspoon garlic powder
½ teaspoon cumin
½ teaspoon onion powder
½ teaspoon sea salt
¼ teaspoon red pepper flakes

1. In a medium pot set over medium heat, heat the coconut oil, coconut flour, and chili powder. Cook for 1 minute so the flour doesn't taste raw.
2. Add the water, tomato paste, garlic powder, cumin, onion powder, salt, and red pepper flakes, to taste. Bring the mixture to a simmer and cook for 25 minutes, stirring occasionally.
3. Serve warm.

Per Serving (½ Cup)
calories: 70 | fat: 3.7g | protein: 1.7g | carbs: 8.4g | fiber: 1.7g

Appendix 1 Measurement Conversion Chart

VOLUME EQUIVALENTS(DRY)

US STANDARD	METRIC (APPROXIMATE)
1/8 teaspoon	0.5 mL
1/4 teaspoon	1 mL
1/2 teaspoon	2 mL
3/4 teaspoon	4 mL
1 teaspoon	5 mL
1 tablespoon	15 mL
1/4 cup	59 mL
1/2 cup	118 mL
3/4 cup	177 mL
1 cup	235 mL
2 cups	475 mL
3 cups	700 mL
4 cups	1 L

VOLUME EQUIVALENTS(LIQUID)

US STANDARD	US STANDARD (OUNCES)	METRIC (APPROXIMATE)
2 tablespoons	1 fl.oz.	30 mL
1/4 cup	2 fl.oz.	60 mL
1/2 cup	4 fl.oz.	120 mL
1 cup	8 fl.oz.	240 mL
1 1/2 cup	12 fl.oz.	355 mL
2 cups or 1 pint	16 fl.oz.	475 mL
4 cups or 1 quart	32 fl.oz.	1 L
1 gallon	128 fl.oz.	4 L

TEMPERATURES EQUIVALENTS

FAHRENHEIT(F)	CELSIUS(C) (APPROXIMATE)
225 °F	107 °C
250 °F	120 °C
275 °F	135 °C
300 °F	150 °C
325 °F	160 °C
350 °F	180 °C
375 °F	190 °C
400 °F	205 °C
425 °F	220 °C
450 °F	235 °C
475 °F	245 °C
500 °F	260 °C

WEIGHT EQUIVALENTS

US STANDARD	METRIC (APPROXIMATE)
1 ounce	28 g
2 ounces	57 g
5 ounces	142 g
10 ounces	284 g
15 ounces	425 g
16 ounces (1 pound)	455 g
1.5 pounds	680 g
2 pounds	907 g

Appendix 2 The Dirty Dozen and Clean Fifteen

The Environmental Working Group (EWG) is a nonprofit, nonpartisan organization dedicated to protecting human health and the environment Its mission is to empower people to live healthier lives in a healthier environment. This organization publishes an annual list of the twelve kinds of produce, in sequence, that have the highest amount of pesticide residue-the Dirty Dozen-as well as a list of the fifteen kinds ofproduce that have the least amount of pesticide residue-the Clean Fifteen.

THE DIRTY DOZEN

- The 2016 Dirty Dozen includes the following produce. These are considered among the year's most important produce to buy organic:

Strawberries	Spinach
Apples	Tomatoes
Nectarines	Bell peppers
Peaches	Cherry tomatoes
Celery	Cucumbers
Grapes	Kale/collard greens
Cherries	Hot peppers

- *The Dirty Dozen list contains two additional itemskale/collard greens and hot peppers-because they tend to contain trace levels of highly hazardous pesticides.*

THE CLEAN FIFTEEN

- The least critical to buy organically are the Clean Fifteen list. The following are on the 2016 list:

Avocados	Papayas
Corn	Kiw
Pineapples	Eggplant
Cabbage	Honeydew
Sweet peas	Grapefruit
Onions	Cantaloupe
Asparagus	Cauliflower
Mangos	

- *Some of the sweet corn sold in the United States are made from genetically engineered (GE) seedstock. Buy organic varieties of these crops to avoid GE produce.*

Appendix 3 3-Week Meal Plan

Week-1	Breakfast	Lunch	Dinner	Snacks/Desserts/Smoothies
Day-1	Mushroom and Onion Risotto	Basil Cashew and Artichoke Lentil Pasta	Squash Pasta with Spaghetti Sauce	Garbanzo and Mushroom "Sausage" Links
Day-2	Herbed Rice Bowl	Watercress and Orange Salad	Spaghetti Squash with Zucchini Pesto	Tarragon Almond Crackers
Day-3	Blackberry Flavor Banana and Quinoa Bars	Mushroom and Bell Pepper Fajitas	Basil Mushroom and Lettuce Burgers	Kale and Avocado
Day-4	Raisin Spelt Cookies	Avocado Spelt Pasta	Apple and Butternut Squash Burger	Nutmeg Date Pudding
Day-5	Chickpea Veg Hot Dogs	Cucumber and Lentil Pasta	Broccoli and Wild Rice Bowl	Peach and Nut Cobbler
Day-6	Quinoa and Chickpea Burgers	Hearty Vegetable Nori Rolls	Lettuce and Zucchini Hummus Wrap	Zucchini Bacon
Day-7	Oat and Walnut Milk Spelt Bread	Zoodles with Tomato-Avocado Sauce	Mushroom and Bell Pepper Fritters	Oregano Almond Breadsticks with Garlic Topping

Week-2	Breakfast	Lunch	Dinner	Snacks/Desserts/Smoothies
Day-1	Amaranth and Zucchini Patties	Bell Pepper and Mushroom Spelt Noodles	Mushroom and Bell Pepper Fajitas	Summer Crisp
Day-2	Date and Kamut Porridge	Herbed Lentil and Potato Coconut Stew	Mushroom and Kale Ravioli	Banana, Date and Walnut Smoothie
Day-3	Vegetable Chickpea Quiche	Tahini Beet Pizza	Pineapple Green Salad	Broccoli Bites

Day-4	Chopped Walnuts with Amaranth	Spaghetti Squash with Zucchini Pesto	Ratatouille	Jicama Fries
Day-5	Walnut Spelt Biscuits	Avocado and Spelt Noodle Salad	Swiss Chard Spelt Pasta	Baked Walnut Apple
Day-6	Amaranth, Zucchini, and Kale Patties	Basil Spinach Pesto Pasta	Mango-Habanero Cauliflower Wraps	Cashew Stuffed Mushrooms
Day-7	Amaranth and Walnut Milk Polenta	Bell Pepper Mushroom Steak	Sweet Tahini Peach Salad	Golden Chickpea Nuggets

Week-3	Breakfast	Lunch	Dinner	Snacks/Desserts/Smoothies
Day-1	Burro Banana Walnut Pancakes	Kale and Chickpea Curry	Broccoli, Asparagus, and Quinoa Salad	Sapote and Nut Pudding
Day-2	Teff Grain Chickpea Burger	Barbecue Sprout Bean Salsa Chili	Broccoli and Carrot Bake	Paprika Almonds
Day-3	Basil Teff Grain Sausage	Broccoli-Basil Pesto Stuffed Sweet Potato	Veg and Quinoa Stuffed Bell Peppers	Tahini Parsley and Zucchini Hummus
Day-4	Amaranth and Quinoa Porridge	Mushroom and Kale Ravioli	Basil Cashew and Artichoke Lentil Pasta	Banana and Blueberry Chia Pudding
Day-5	Mushroom and Pepper Chickpea Loaf	Squash Pasta with Spaghetti Sauce	Chickpea, Bell Pepper and Mushroom Curry	Avocado and Cucumber Sushi Roll
Day-6	Banana Muffin with Walnuts	Herbed Lentil and Potato Coconut Stew	Spaghetti Squash with Zucchini Pesto	Coconut and Vanilla Bean Sundae
Day-7	Blueberry, Banana, and Amaranth Pancakes	Broccoli, Asparagus, and Quinoa Salad	Avocado and Spelt Noodle Salad	Hearty Party Snack Mix

Appendix 4 Recipe Index

Made in the USA
Columbia, SC
29 June 2025

60071036R00067